Mindful Moods

a mindful, social emotional learning curriculum for grades 3-5

2nd Edition

Wynne Kinder, M. Ed.

WynneKinder.com

WellnessWorksinSchools.com

Published by Oxford Southern Press
an imprint of Sunbury Press, Inc.
Mechanicsburg, Pennsylvania

Copyright © 2017, 2020 by Wynne Kinder, M. Ed.
Cover copyright © 2020 by Wynne Kinder.

Sunbury Press supports copyright. Copyright fuels creativity, encourages diverse voices, promotes free speech, and creates a vibrant culture. Thank you for buying an authorized edition of this book and for complying with copyright laws by not reproducing, scanning, or distributing any part of it in any form without permission. You are supporting writers and allowing Sunbury Press to continue to publish books for every reader. For information contact Sunbury Press, Inc., Subsidiary Rights Dept., PO Box 548, Boiling Springs, PA 17011 USA or legal@sunburypress.com.

For information about special discounts for bulk purchases, please contact Sunbury Press Orders Dept. at (855) 338-8359 or orders@sunburypress.com.

To request one of our authors for speaking engagements or book signings, please contact Sunbury Press Publicity Dept. at publicity@sunburypress.com.

FIRST OXFORD SOUTHERN PRESS EDITION: June 2020
Publisher's Cataloging-in-Publication Data
Names: Kinder, Wynne, author.
Title: Mindful Moods : a mindful, social emotional learning curriculum for grades 3-5 / by Wynne Kinder, M. Ed.
Description: 2nd paperback edition. | Mechanicsburg, PA : Sunbury Press, 2020.
Summary: Educational teacher curriculum for grades 3-5.
Identifiers: ISBN 978-1-62006-397-2 (softcover)
Subjects: | BISAC: EDUCATION / curricula. | EDUCATION / Behavioral Management. | EDUCATION / Elementary.

Set in Perpetua
Designed by Chris Fenwick | Cover by Jessica Mauger | Edited by Chris Fenwick

GoNoodle name and logo are trademarks of GoNoodle Inc. All GoNoodle Channels, Videos, Names, and Activities are copyrighted by GoNoodle Inc. Used with permission. 209 10th Avenue South, Suite 350, Nashville, TN 37203

Product of the United States of America
0 1 1 2 3 5 8 13 21 34 55

Continue the Enlightenment!

TABLE OF CONTENTS

INTRODUCTION	01
Mindful Practices in Schools	01
Social Emotional Learning in Schools	02
Mindfulness/Social Emotional Learning Together	02
Trauma Informed Teaching Practices	03
TEACHING GUIDE	04
Preparation	04
Planning and Pacing	09
Guided Worksheet for Teachers	10
MODULE 1: It's All You	11
Module Map	12
Lesson 1: Aware	14
Lesson 2: Awake	22
Lesson 3: Care	30
Lesson 4: Rest	38
MODULE 2: Name It & Tame It	47
Module Map	48
Lesson 1: Name It	50
Lesson 2: Weigh It	58
Lesson 3: Feel It	66
Lesson 4: Tame It	74
MODULE 3: Helpful Emotions	83
Module Map	84

Lesson 1: Emotions Speak	86
Lesson 2: Angry Fists	94
Lesson 3: Worried Belly	102
Lesson 4: Knots of Emotions	110

MODULE 4: Bump & Bounce Back — 119

Module Map	120
Lesson 1: Setbacks & Bumps	122
Lesson 2: Self Talk	130
Lesson 3: Bounce Back	138
Lesson 4: Begin Again	146

ACTIVITY SHEETS — 155

RESOURCES: Mindfulness for Schools — 162

INFO: Wellness Works in Schools / Wynne Kinder — 163

INTRODUCTION

Mindful Practices in Schools

Mindfulness has been defined in many ways. One definition might be: paying attention to the present moment, with openness and compassion. Another is: single tasking. Yet another: What emerges when we attend to the present moment in a particular way.

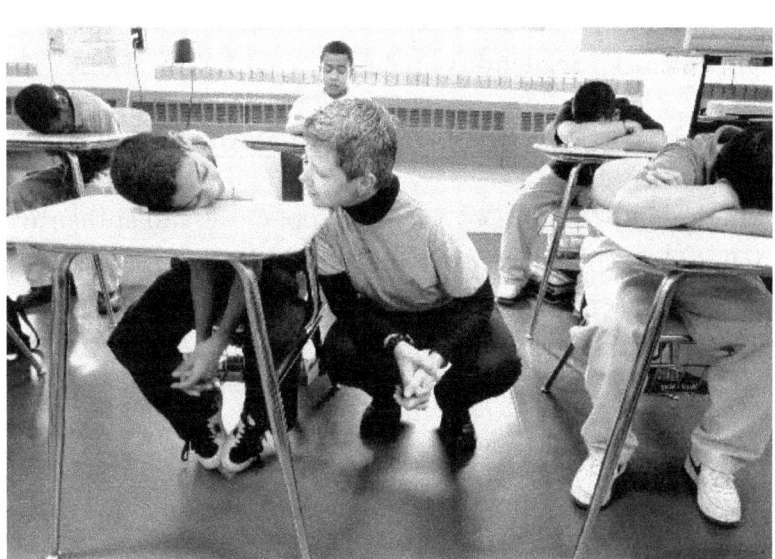

Most approaches to being mindful or practicing it include purposeful mindful practices that train attention - to select, direct, and sustain focus. Awareness can be enhanced, especially when the target of attention is on oneself–thoughts, emotions, sensations in the body, breath, and other sensory input. To create comfort, we can utilize more familiar targets of focus, such as visual, auditory, and physical experiences as well. Over time one may notice clearer thoughts, increased emotional regulation, and a sense of balance.

Repeated present-moment awareness at all ages may be simple *and* challenging at the same time. Consistent mindful practices in the classroom can lead to changes in self-awareness, self-care, emotion regulation, concentration, and mental flexibility, which can all enhance performance in school and out.

The practices might be still, active, individualized, synchronized, loud, quiet, calm, or energized. Mindful movement is becoming more and more useful in reaching and engaging diverse populations and wide-ranging age groups.

Mindfulness and the practices that are inspired by it, typically have a similar foundation and intention but can look different from one classroom to another and from one day to another. Definitions and expressions can take many turns depending on the teacher, the group of students, and the diverse needs of each classroom. When teachers try them out and make the practices *their own*, mindfulness can become a powerful personal habit and an invaluable gift that we give to our students.

Social Emotional Learning in Schools

Social Emotional Learning (SEL) is typically one's contribution to classroom and community culture. It begins with naming and understanding the social aspects of interactions as well as the information emotions give us. Empathy, negotiating the world around us, and getting along with others are common goals of SEL programming. When we learn specific these SEL skills as steppingstones for healthy interactions, the by-product is a more harmonious learning space, often valued by students and teachers alike. Self-awareness and self-regulation are foundational to SEL programming. Desired outcomes for SEL are often: emotional regulation, prosocial interactions, and enhanced academic outcomes.

Mindfulness and Social Emotional Learning (MSEL) – Together

Mindfulness encourages a sense of openness and authenticity, often required to take on the activities involved in social emotional learning. Some may see little difference between mindfulness skills and social emotional learning within the classroom setting. But a simple delineation is that mindfulness is working from the inside out. And social emotional learning is working from the outside in.

It seems logical to see that the social aspects of life are focused on our skillful interactions with the outside (with others) and that mindfulness, with its predominance for self-awareness and self-care, focuses on one's inner life. But what about the emotional learning portion of SEL? Emotional awareness and regulation have such a personal source. How can that come from the outside? It might seem like a nuance, but it is important for this discussion.

Mindfulness is working from the inside out and Social Emotional Learning is working from the outside in.

Family attitudes toward handling emotions, supported within counseling and personal therapy, provide individualized strategies for managing the most intense of emotions. SEL does not aim to replace or delve into the counseling-based approach to emotions. It instead, aims to educate students about emotions and introduce them to accessible/universal means of managing them.

Combining SEL with Mindfulness helps us see that therapy asks, "How are you feeling right now? What could have caused that feeling?" and MSEL asks, "People feel lots of emotions, which ones can you see in the way they stand? Or "how does your body let you know that you are worried?"

So, when it comes to foundational understanding and awareness of emotions, it is useful for feelings to be perceived as universal and mentionable. Working from the outside in, in terms of emotions, encourages empathy and understanding of others' inner lives, as well as our own. In this curriculum, mindfulness (working from the inside out) is laid as a foundation from which social emotional awareness and skills can grow. We are, therefore, utilizing practices like attention to breath and safe movement while honoring the experience of others. "If social emotional learning is a house, then mindfulness is its foundation."

Mindful Moods — a mindful, social emotional learning curriculum for grades 3-5

This curriculum integrates SEL educational standards by introducing and exploring a wide range of emotions, as well as the social awareness related to others' experience of emotions. It explores the impact of emotions on self (physiology and behavior) then on our relationships with others. It includes introductory practices of mindful awareness, social skills, emotion awareness, and regulation. **Mindful Moods** lays the developmentally appropriate groundwork for integrating mindfulness skills as self-care tools along with strategies that enhance social emotional learning.

Trauma-Informed Teaching Practices

Mindful Moods introduces the trauma-informed lens through which effective and compassionate teachers see those living with old pain. We as teachers need to all but assume there is *trauma in the room*, and act, speak and respond based on that. This trauma-informed approach is embedded in these lessons, scripts, components, activities, and practices.

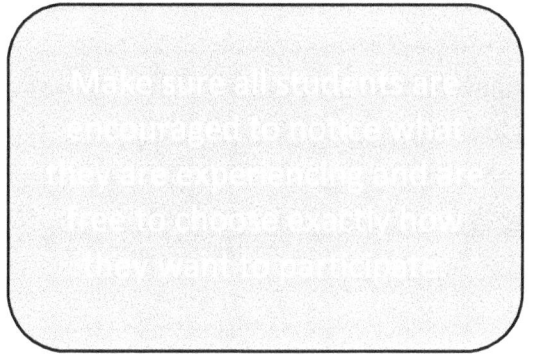

Choice has emerged as the most powerful thread weaving through this approach. Simply put – trauma occurred in a choice-less moment, where/when an event overwhelmed one's own inner resources. Re-inviting *choice* into the lives of all children allows for comfort, efficacy, and less triggering.

First, do no harm. Begin there when asking anyone to notice and even delve into the most well-protected aspects of their lives (i.e., emotions, thoughts, relationships, and bodily sensations).

Second, explicitly teach *choice*. Teachers never need to rationalize why choice is helpful, just that it is, for all. We can make sure <u>all</u> students are encouraged to notice what they are experiencing and are **free to choose** exactly how they want to participate. As an example, teachers can use invitational language (i.e., "can, might, try, notice") and continually encourage diverse expressions of participation in activities and accept/reinforce varied demonstrations of knowledge.

Choice as an Instructional Tool

Offering choice, when teaching **Mindful Moods,** might look like this: students choose where to sit, how to sit, when to join the group, or when/how to be in the audience, until comfortable. Choice sounds like *invitational language* when giving directives to the group:

- give it a try; it will look different for each of us
- sit quietly, listen, and watch carefully, so you are ready to join us in a bit
- choose what you do and let others participate
- stay with us and join in when you feel ready
- move to a safe chair/space in the room and watch from there.

TEACHING GUIDE

Learning Modules – 4 lessons in each

The four learning modules provide a big picture of the curriculum. They are organized by theme (It's All You, Name It & Tame It, Helpful Emotions, and Bump & Bounce Back) and are taught in groups of four lessons. Best practice is to teach one lesson each week for 16 weeks. Of course, there are many ways to arrange, rearrange, and deliver the instruction based on the needs of students and style their teacher.

Mindful Message: This message weaves through the 4-lesson Learning Module and ties together the 4 lessons within. Reiterate the message for students as often as needed throughout the lessons. Writing it on the board may be helpful as a reminder.

Module Map – a curriculum map for each module

The 2-page spread **module map** provides a curriculum overview, outlines activities, and helps divide the four learning modules into four groups of four lessons (16 lessons in total). The map for each **learning module** gives teachers a bird's eye view of what will happen throughout the four lessons. Goals, preparation ideas, SEL connections, materials, and video options are on the Teaching Preparation (PREP) page.

And the Teaching Components (TEACH) page includes the 5 components of teaching each lesson: focus, mindful moves, explore, balance, and rest.

Some practices and activities vary from lesson to lesson, while most aspects will repeat within the module. *Challenges* are integrated to create a balance between novelty and comforting familiarity.

The structure of the lessons is created to be very predictable and teachable. As you look through the pages to get to know the curriculum, you will notice repetition. That repetition will create comfort for you and your students.

Teaching Preparation

Page 1 of each lesson

Goal refers to the concepts or skills that teachers wish for their students to understand or do.

SEL Connection mentions the aspect of the lesson that connects with social emotional learning.

Teaching Tools outline what will be needed for instruction.

Title of Lesson
Goal
SEL Connection
Teaching Tools
Materials
Pre-Practice
Videos

Materials (1 per classroom): chimes, magnifying glass, feather, stone, super bouncy ball, and piece of string/rope.

    Gathering/Shopping List: <u>Have</u>   <u>Need</u>

Classroom Tools (for each student): There are a few classroom tools that teachers will want available: a chalkboard (or something like it), index cards, paper, pencils, and crayons.

    Gathering/Shopping List: <u>Have</u>   <u>Need</u>

Activity Sheets: included in the resources section of each curriculum book and can be reproduced.

    Print/Copy List: <u>Lesson?</u>   <u>When?</u>

Pre-Practice: This "apple for the teacher" is a gentle and supportive suggestion for you, as a way of *taking care of yourself first* and then being more prepared to create a healthy mindset to lead Mindful Moods lessons.

See **Resources: Mindfulness for Teachers** at the end of this manual for more ideas.

What have you found?

<u>Books</u>   <u>Articles</u>   <u>Websites</u>   <u>Apps</u>   <u>Colleagues to ask</u>

<u>Videos</u> by GoNoodle and Wynne Kinder

With GoNoodle, Wynne wrote, co-created, and recorded dozens of educational, mindful videos for elementary students. Those mindful videos have reached millions of young people in their classrooms and in their homes (*GoNoodleKids App*). **Mindful SEL Channels** include: FLOW, THINK ABOUT IT, and some on BLAZER Fresh, totaling 50+ videos.

Most of the mindful videos are free to teachers, kids, and families. A few are included only in *GoNoodle PLUS* (annual fee), which expands access. The links to many of these kid-safe videos are found within the **Mindful Moods** lessons themselves. GoNoodle continually changes which videos are in *PLUS*, so check ahead of time.

These videos are purely **optional** possibilities for diversifying the presentation of material, enriching the experience, providing extra practice, and expanding on an activity. Prior to teaching a lesson, open each lesson-specific video in a separate tab, within your browser, so they are ready to go. You may want to try them yourself first.

Try out GoNoodle on your own first. Explore the free version and find out how much is available to you and your students. Just register for your classroom, pick a Champ, and try the practices.

Also look for **Spanish language versions** being created monthly by GoNoodle.

FLOW:

Think About It:

BLAZER Fresh:

Teaching Components

These components provide a predictable structure within each lesson and allow for ease of planning. Grouping by component and by pages (6 pages per lesson) gives each teacher the freedom to choose. You can divide lessons or spread lessons across instructional blocks or even across days in a week.

Page 2 of each lesson

FOCUS is an opening routine to settle the bodies and focus the attention of the group.

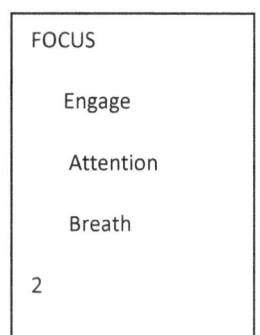

- **Engage** – Before ringing the chimes to practice attention and awareness, it will be helpful to provide context, invite curiosity, or kindle interest within your students. One option is a 3-minute video or quick review linked to the lesson topic.
- **Attention** – Practice directing and sustaining attention on the sound of chimes and beyond.
- **Breath Practice** – This component introduces the target of attention being the *breath*, rather than a sound. Notice a few subtle changes in the directions between modules and lessons to increase novelty.

Pages 3 and 4 of each lesson

MINDFUL MOVES – Moving the body while paying attention to self (to one's own needs and personal comfort) makes for a safer experience. Mindful movement can release stress as well as energize the mind and body. Videos are sometimes included.

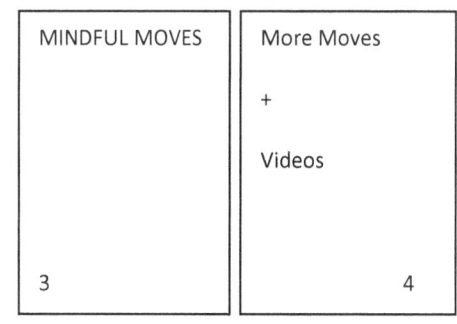

We have added ***Challenges** to repeated Moves that will diversify the experience.

Create Your Own *Challenges _____

Feel free to create your own *Challenges too. As your class experiences the lessons and practices, students will feel increasingly empowered to explore, adapt, and rename many of the classics like *Elevator Breath* can become *Skyscraper Breath* by reaching higher and/or standing up.

Have a pen ready to record/brainstorm in this manual, add any ideas that arise.

Page 5 of each lesson

EXPLORE – Explore the content and skills in the lesson through group/individual activities, *Think-Pair-Share*, and Solo Reflections.

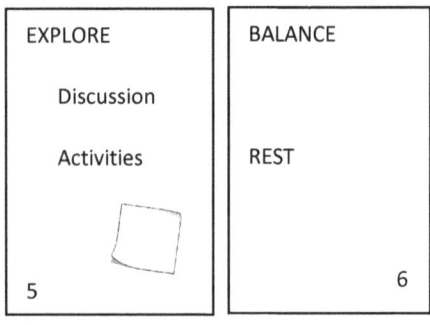

Sticky Notes are printed within each lesson for teachers to jot down ideas for the next lesson, their own noticings, reminders, extension options, changes for future practice, and "I wish I had…"

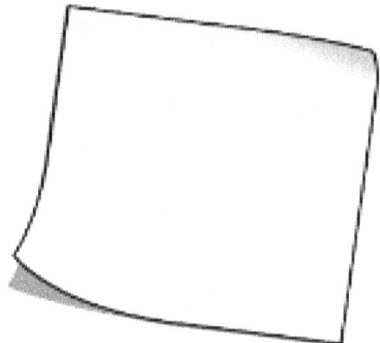

Page 6 of each lesson

BALANCE - The balance activity combines the skills of **focus and regulation** into a real-life experience. Success is experienced when we attempt, adjust, and try again. We can honor one's ability to safely fade out, fall out, pause, regroup – then regain focus, become steady, and try again. And again.

REST – Resting is often a challenge for both students and teachers. The mindful practice in this portion sets the group up for even a few moments to practice resting. It is a practice, not a performance.

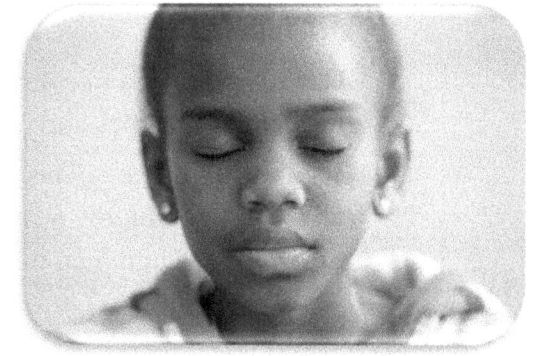

Page 7 and 8 of each lesson

Lesson Reflection for Teaching Mindful Moods

Throughout the teaching of Mindful Moods, teachers often find it helpful to plan, record, remind, and reflect as they go. The last two pages of each lesson provide space and structure for that routine.

Try reflecting here:

What is your initial impression of how this curriculum will be for you?

_____

What are you looking forward to? _____

What is something you want to learn? _____

Planning, Spacing, and Pacing

Depending on what teachers notice about the readiness of their students, planning can be very individualized, condensed, expanded, or divided. Even the order of the components can be adjusted, per lesson, or throughout the program. Some **possibilities** for dividing, pacing, spacing, and ordering the components or pages are listed below.

> **Week-long Option** – 4 blocks/days during *Morning Meetings*, 10-15 minutes each:
>
> Monday – **FOCUS** with video
>
> Tuesday – Review (video reminder) + **MINDFUL MOVES**
>
> Wednesday – Favorite MINDFUL MOVE with video + **EXPLORE**
>
> Friday – **BALANCE & REST**
>
> **Two-Day Option** – during 2 *Social Skills Blocks*, 30 minutes each:
>
> Wednesday – **FOCUS** + **MINDFUL MOVES**
>
> Thursday – **EXPLORE** + **BALANCE & REST**
>
> **Single-Block Option** – during 45-minute block within one day:
>
> One lesson in one block with a break between **MINDFUL MOVES** and **EXPLORE**
>
> Ideas: _____
> _____

Changing the **order** of the components is a helpful possibility. Maybe a group does well with trying out the more active video first, then the EXPLORE activity fits, followed by BALANCE & REST. The remainder of the lesson can fall into place from there.

Repeating means practicing. Practicing means repeating. Feel free to repeat the Engage portion, the Balances, or any video as needed. Repetition and following the requests of students will also increase engagement and participation.

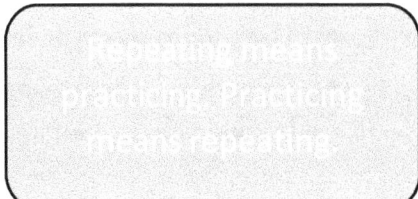

Repeating means practicing. Practicing means repeating.

Mindful Moods *a guided worksheet for Teachers*

Mindset of Success: Practice ways to ready yourself for teaching, guiding, and supporting.

    Teacher's Intentions: What are yours? _____

    Personal Practice: What is your go-to practice? _____

        What practices have you found helpful? daily? _____

Prepare: Set up your room, inform your students, and share resources with their families.

    Classroom: How will your room be arranged? _____

    Students: What will you tell them ahead of time? _____

    Parents: Email or message before you start? _____

Plan: Make a plan for pacing and timing. Be realistic and keep it simple.

    16 lessons fit into our school day: _____ on _____

    How might you adjust the plan? _____

    Ideas for adaptations based on interests and needs of your group? _____

    Provide *Choice*: Write them down before starting. _____

Differentiate Instruction: You know your students and their needs.

    What do you already do, for whom?_____

_____

_____

- Write ideas/concepts/mindful messages/reminders/mindful moves on paper or the board.
- Use videos more or less often based on the needs and interests of your students.
- Provide *extension options* for students and families through accessible resources like books, videos, GoNoodle digital brain breaks, and <u>GoNoodleKids</u> App for home.

Module 1

It's All You

Mindful Message: When we practice paying attention to what we feel in our bodies, we choose wisely and can take better care of ourselves.

Teaching Preparation for Module 1

LESSON GOAL	SEL CONNECTION	TEACHING TOOLS	GoNoodle VIDEOS
Lesson 1 **Aware** Students practice noticing sensations in their bodies.	Become aware of the sensations we all might feel and build empathy for others along the way.	**Materials:** Chimes Magnifying glass **Pre-Practice:** Belly Breath	**Videos:** FLOW – *from Mindless to Mindful* FLOW – *Rainbow Breath*
Lesson 2 **Awake** Students practice shifting energy to be more alert and awake.	Practice regulating personal energy and emotions.	**Materials:** Chimes Index cards & pencils **Pre-Practice:** Belly Breath	**Videos:** FLOW – *Up & Moving* MAXIMO – *Propeller* BLAZER FRESH – *Fit the Sitch*
Lesson 3 **Care** Students recognize how it feels to be safe and care for themselves	Begin to empathize with other's needs for self-care.	**Materials:** Chimes **Pre-Practice:** 2-Handed Belly Breath	**Videos:** FLOW – *On & Off* FLOW – *Rainbow Breath* THINK ABOUT IT – *Rest Well*
Lesson 4 **Rest** Students practice shifting energy to settle and rest.	Recognize and create a feeling of safety.	**Materials:** Chimes Paper & pencil **Pre-Practice:** 2-Handed Belly Breath	**Videos:** THINK ABOUT IT – *Find Peace* THINK ABOUT IT – *Rest Well*

Teaching Components for Module 1

FOCUS	MINDFUL MOVES	EXPLORE	BALANCE & REST
Engage: Video FLOW – *from Mindless to Mindful* **Attention:** Chimes **Breath:** Belly Breath	Mindful Mountain Hand Jive Mindful Circles Rainbow Breath **Video:** FLOW – *Rainbow Breath*	**Chalk Talk:** Sensations we notice in the body - comfortable or uncomfortable?	**Balance:** Bent Arrow **Rest:** 2-Handed Belly Breath
Engage: Video FLOW – *Up & Moving* **Attention:** Chimes **Breath:** Belly Breath	Mindful Mountain Hand Jive Mindful Circles Rainbow Breath	**Think-Pair-Share:** Explore ideas for raising energy	**Balance:** Bent Arrow **Rest:** 2-Handed Belly Breath **Videos:** BLAZER Fresh – *Fit the Sitch*

Engage: Video
 	
FLOW – *On & Off*
 	
Attention: Chimes
 	
Breath: Belly Breath
	Mindful Mountain Hand Jive
	Mindful Circles
	   with *Challenge
	Rainbow Breath
	
	Video:
	FLOW –
	Rainbow Breath
		Group Activity:
		
		This or That's
			Balance:
			Bent Arrow
			   with *Challenge
			
			Rest:
			Seated Plank
			
			Video:
			THINK ABOUT IT –
			Rest Well

Engage: Video
 	
THINK ABOUT IT -
Find Peace
 	
Attention: Chimes
 	
Breath: Belly Breath
	Mindful Mountain Hand Jive
	   with *Challenge
	Mindful Circles
	   with *Challenge
	Rainbow Breath
		Solo Reflection:
		
		Guide statement and questions
			Balance:
			Bent Arrow
			   with *Challenge
			
			Rest:
			Seated Plank
			
			Video:
			THINK ABOUT IT –
			Rest Well

| Module 1 — It's All You | **Mindful Message:** When we practice paying attention to what we feel in our bodies, we can choose wisely and take better care of ourselves. |

Lesson 1 - Aware

Goal: Students practice noticing sensations in their bodies.

Materials:

- Chimes
- Magnifying glass

Pre-Practice

Belly Breath

SEL Connection:

Become *aware* of the sensations we all feel and build empathy for others along the way.

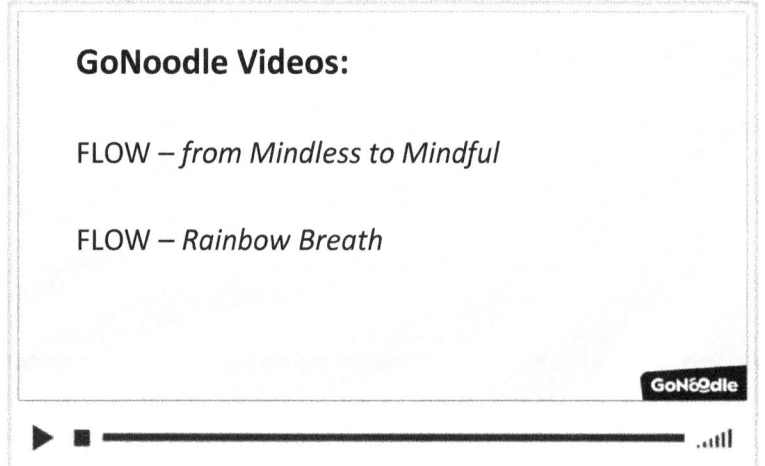

GoNoodle Videos:

FLOW – *from Mindless to Mindful*

FLOW – *Rainbow Breath*

FOCUS

Engage: Video

FLOW - *from Mindless to Mindful*

Attention: Chimes

Place your attention on the sound.

Ring Chime 1 time.

Be still for the next two sounds.

Ring chime 2 times.

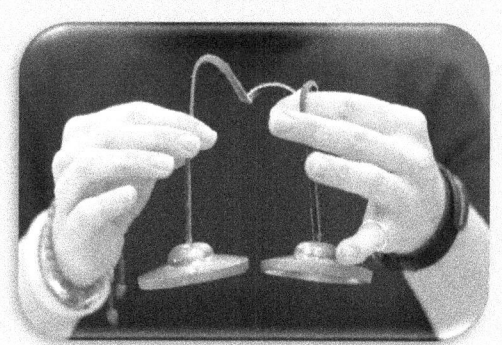

Breath: Belly Breath

Place one hand on your belly.

Model remaining still and noticing movement in the belly for two breaths.

Gently stare at a spot or close your eyes for 2 more Belly Breaths.

MINDFUL MOVES

We all get to move by CHOICE.
Notice how your body feels and decide how you wish to sit then move.

Mindful Mountain

Put a picture of a mountain in your mind:

    a tall peak with gentle slopes,

    sitting solidly and still on the ground.

Sit tall, shoulders down, settle in, hands rest,

    muscles soften, eyes close or stare.

Be a mindful mountain.

Hand Jive

Sit comfortably.

Wring hands as if washing them.

Slowly, then quickly.

Wiggle fingers. Open and close. Pause.

Circle closed fists. Circle open hands.

Try same directions, different

    directions, quickly, slowly and then in super-slow motion.

Hands in lap, now rest.

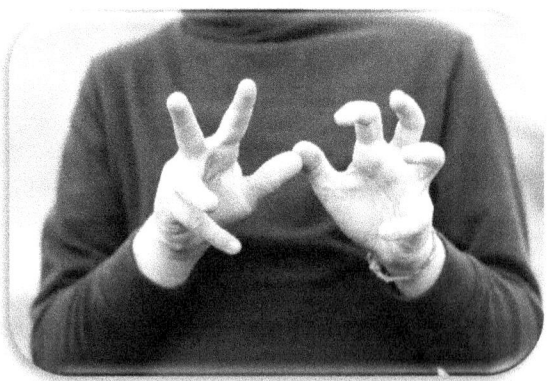

Mindful Circles

Sit tall and relaxed.

Notice how it feels to circle each at your own pace.

- Head
- Shoulders
- Ribs
- Ankles

Try moving in one direction, then the other.

Rainbow Breath

Sit strong and relaxed.

Hands reach down at sides.

Breathe in to reach wide, then up.

Pause.

Breathe out to float arms wide and down.

Repeat with breath two more times.

GoNoodle Video:

FLOW – *Rainbow Breath*

EXPLORE

Chalk Talk:

- Write this title on the board: ***Sensations in the Body***
- What you feel might be small or hard to notice. Let's focus (look closely) with this tool – magnifying glass.
- Draw two columns (T chart) under title.
- Label one ***"uncomfortable"*** and the other ***"comfortable."***
- Discussion/Guide Questions:

"In your opinion, what do you feel in your body when it is uncomfortable?"

>Sample answers: *sore, tight, yucky, tired, achy, swollen*

"What in your body feels comfortable?"

>Sample answers: *loose, strong, rested, energized, ready, ease*

- Wrap-Up: *When we notice closely and carefully (like with this magnifying glass) what we feel in our bodies, we can start to find healthy ways to take good care of ourselves.*

Reflection: Ask students for verbal reflections.

BALANCE

Bent Arrow Balance

Sit on a chair or on the floor.

Sit tall and try not to lean back.

Stare at a spot in front of you.

Lift one bent leg, hold with same hand under knee.

Bend and lift the other leg too. Pause.

Focus and stay steady. Breathe.

Adjust and begin again, if needed.

Stay for 5, 4, 3, 2, 1.

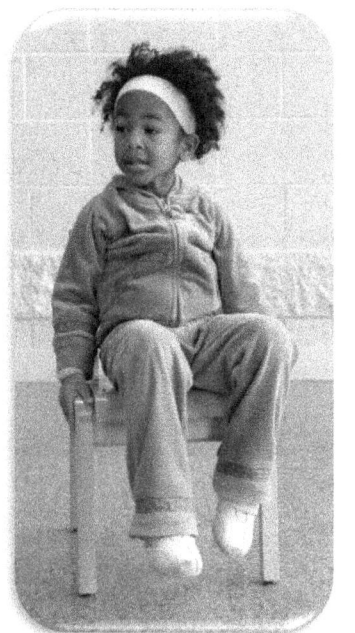

REST

2-Handed Belly Breath

Place both hands open on belly.

Notice your belly move with a few breaths.

Eyes are open or closed.

*Settle in and **Rest**.*

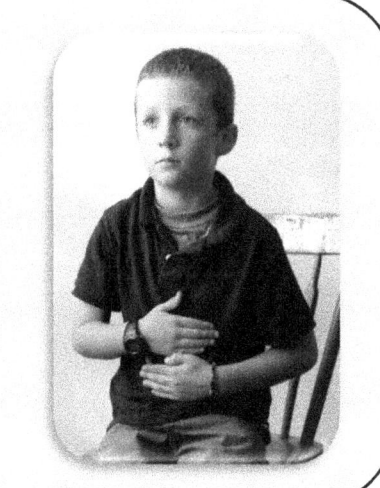

Lesson Reflection for Teaching Mindful Moods

Highlights

What did students report / notice?

What did you notice, for you or for students?

Components

What aspects can you repeat as a practice, beyond the lesson?

What can you change to be more relevant for your students?

What can be tied in and integrated into other subjects or themes?

Planning, Spacing & Pacing

How did the timing play a role in the experience of the lesson?

What will you adjust for next lesson or next year?

Resources & Materials

What worked well?

What didn't quite fit?

What will you look for / research / have on hand next time?

What additional materials would be helpful for the next lesson?

And for this lesson next year?

Teacher Reflection

What is your overall impression of your experience of this lesson / module?

Module 1
It's All You

Mindful Message:
When we practice paying attention to what we feel in our bodies, we can choose wisely and take better care of ourselves.

Lesson 2 - Awake

Goal: Students practice shifting energy to be more alert and awake.

Materials:

- Chimes
- Index cards & pencils

Pre-Practice

Belly Breath

SEL Connection:

Practice regulating personal energy and emotions.

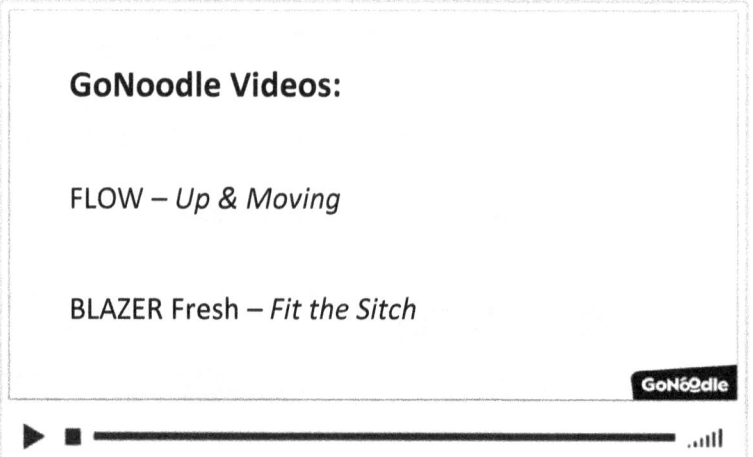

GoNoodle Videos:

FLOW – *Up & Moving*

BLAZER Fresh – *Fit the Sitch*

FOCUS

Engage: Video option

FLOW - *Up & Moving*

Attention: Chimes

Place your attention on the sound.

Ring Chime 1 time.

Be still for the next two sounds.

Ring chime 2 times.

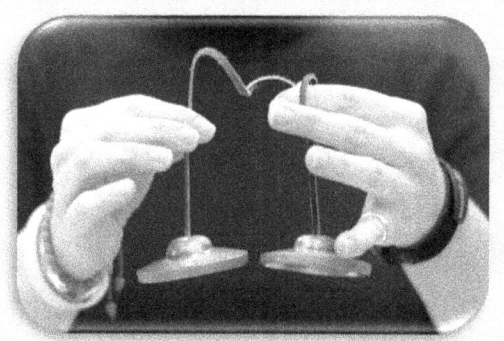

Breath: Belly Breath

Place one hand on your belly.

Model remaining still and noticing movement

in the belly for two breaths.

Gently stare at a spot or close your eyes for 2 more belly breaths.

MINDFUL MOVES

**We all get to move by CHOICE.
Notice how your body feels and decide how to move.**

Mindful Mountain

Put a picture of a mountain in your mind:

    a tall peak with gentle slopes,

    sitting solidly and still on the ground.

Sit tall, shoulders down, settle in, hands rest,

    muscles soften, eyes close or stare.

Be a mindful mountain.

Hand Jive

Sit comfortably.

Wring hands as if washing them.

Slowly, then quickly.

Wiggle fingers. Open and close. Pause.

Circle closed fists. Circle open hands.

Try same directions, different

    directions, quickly, slowly and then in super-slow motion.

Hands in lap, rest.

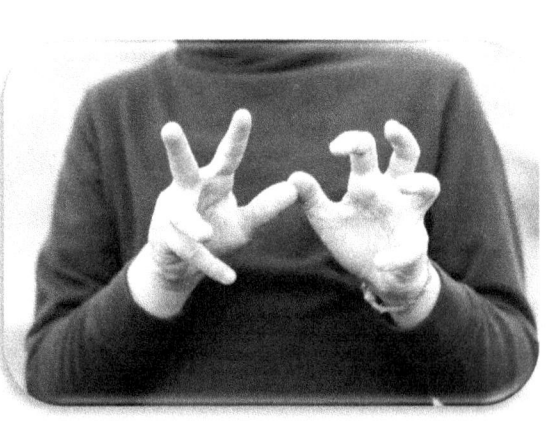

Mindful Circles

Sit tall and relaxed.

Notice how it feels to circle each at your own pace.

- Head
- Shoulders
- Ribs
- Ankles

Try moving in one direction, then the other.

Rainbow Breath

Sit strong and relaxed.

Arms hang down at sides.

Breathe in to reach wide and up.

Pause.

Breathe out to float arms wide and down.

Repeat with breath two more times.

Imagine that a rainbow forms above you, either going up or while going down.

EXPLORE

Think-Pair-Share

All students will need an index card and a pencil.

Guide Question:

> *"Imagine what it is like to feel low energy or tired.*
>
> *Now, **THINK** of three things you can do you need to raise your energy - to be more awake and alert."*

Students write or draw pictures of 2-3 ideas on index card.

Sample Ideas: *Go outside, eat a snack, do rainbow breath...*

PAIR and SHARE with a partner.

Option: Share / compare with whole group.

GoNoodle Video:

BLAZER Fresh – *Fit the Sitch*

Reflection: Ask students for verbal reflections.

BALANCE

Bent Arrow Balance

Sit on a chair or on the floor.

Sit tall and try not to lean back.

Stare at a spot in front of you.

Lift one bent leg, hold with same hand under knee.

Bend and lift the other leg. Pause. Breathe.

Focus and stay steady. Maybe straighten legs.

Adjust and begin again, if needed.

Stay for 5, 4, 3, 2, 1.

REST

2-Handed Belly Breath

Place both hands open on belly.

Notice your belly move with a few breaths.

Eyes are open or closed.

Settle in and **Rest**.

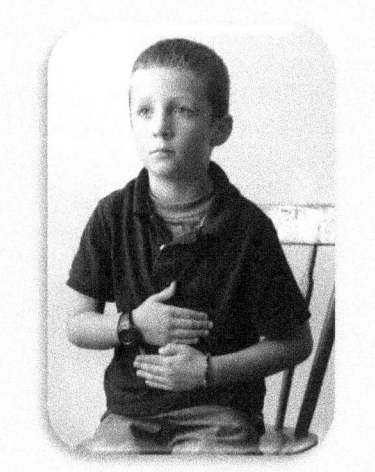

Lesson Reflection for Teaching Mindful Moods

Highlights

What did students report / notice?

What did you notice, for you or for students?

Components

What aspects can you repeat as a practice, beyond the lesson?

What can you change to be more relevant for your students?

What can be tied in and integrated into other subjects or themes?

Planning, Spacing & Pacing

How did the timing play a role in the experience of the lesson?

What will you adjust for next lesson or next year?

Resources & Materials

What worked well?

What didn't quite fit?

What will you look for / research / have on hand next time?

What additional materials would be helpful for the next lesson?

And for this lesson next year?

Teacher Reflection

What is your overall impression of your experience of this lesson / module?

Module 1 **It's All You**	**Mindful Message:** When we practice paying attention to what we feel in our bodies, we can choose wisely and take better care of ourselves.

Lesson 3 - Care

Goal: Students recognize how it feels to be safe and care for themselves.

Materials:

- Chimes

Pre-Practice

2-Handed Belly Breath

SEL Connection:

Begin to empathize with other's needs for self-care.

GoNoodle Videos:

FLOW – *On & Off*

FLOW – *Rainbow Breath*

THINK ABOUT IT – *Rest Well*

FOCUS

Engage: Video option

FLOW - *On & Off*

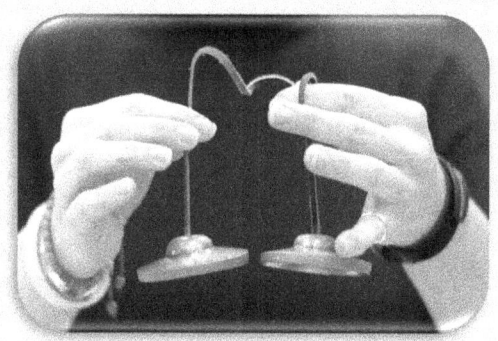

Attention: Chimes

Place your attention on the sound.

Ring Chime 1 time.

Be still for the next two sounds.

Ring chime 2 times.

Breath: Belly Breath

Place one hand on your belly.

Model remaining still and noticing movement

In the belly for two breaths.

Gently stare at a spot or close your eyes for 2 more Belly Breaths.

MINDFUL MOVES

**We all get to move by CHOICE.
Notice how your body feels and decide how to sit and how to move.**

Mindful Mountain

Put a picture of a mountain in your mind:

    a tall peak with gentle slopes,

    sitting solidly and still on the ground.

Sit tall, shoulders down, settle in, hands rest,

    muscles soften, eyes close or stare.

Be a mindful mountain.

Hand Jive

Sit comfortably.

Wring hands as if washing them.

Slowly, then quickly.

Wiggle fingers. Open and close. Pause.

Circle closed fists. Circle open hands.

Try same directions, different

    directions, quickly, slowly and super-slow motion.

Hands in lap, rest.

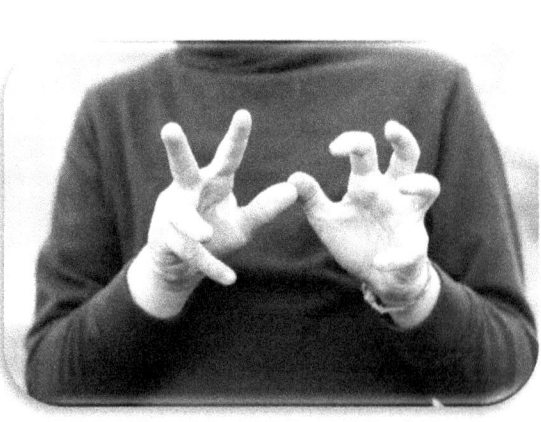

Mindful Circles*

Sit tall and relaxed.

Notice how it feels to circle each at your own pace.

- Shoulders
- *Elbows
- *Fingers
- *Big Toes

Try moving, circling in one direction, then try in the other direction.

Rainbow Breath

Sit strong and relaxed.

Arms hang down at sides.

Breathe in to reach arms wide and up.

Pause.

Breathe out to float arms wide and down.

Repeat with breath two more times but

try more slowly for these two.

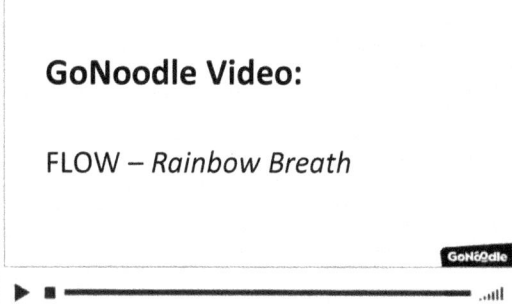

GoNoodle Video:

FLOW – *Rainbow Breath*

EXPLORE

Group Activity

THIS or THATS

Students consider their own the options, their own preference and then take care to vote for themselves (by raising hands).

Would you choose THIS or THAT…?

- Pet a porcupine or feed an eagle?
- Be able to stop time or fly?
- Sleep outside in the woods or sleep outside at the beach?
- Spend the day surfing the internet or surfing in the ocean?
- Sit inside or play outside?
- Give a gift or receive a gift?
- Take the elevator or hike the stairs?
- _____
- _____
- _____

Reflection:

Ask students for verbal reflections.

Noticings?

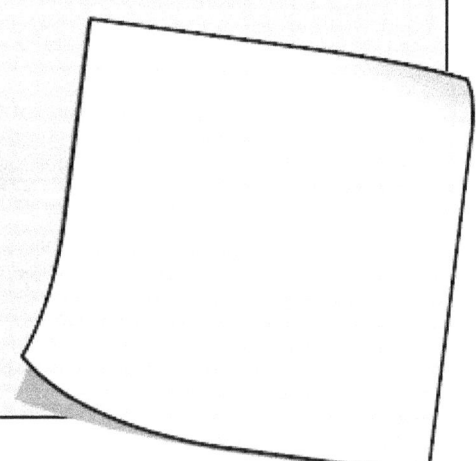

BALANCE

Bent Arrow Balance

Sit tall in a chair or on the floor.

Stare at a spot in front of you.

Lift one bent leg and hold, add other leg.

Focus and stay steady. Breathe.

Adjust and begin again, if needed.

> ***Challenge:*** *No Hands - notice if you want to try letting go of your legs. If not, it's okay. Maybe just one at a time.*

Adjust and repeat.

REST

Seated Plank

Lean back in your chair.

Stretch your legs long and point your toes.

Extend arms up and behind, reach.

Make your body as straight as a plank
    but remain comfortable.

Maybe yawn.

Settle and stay for a few breaths.

Rest.

GoNoodle Video:

THINK ABOUT IT – *Rest Well*

Lesson Reflection for Teaching Mindful Moods

Highlights

What did students report / notice?

What did you notice, for you or for students?

Components

What aspects can you repeat as a practice, beyond the lesson?

What can you change to be more relevant for your students?

What can be tied in and integrated into other subjects or themes?

Planning, Spacing & Pacing

How did the timing play a role in the experience of the lesson?

What will you adjust for next lesson or next year?

Resources & Materials

What worked well?

What didn't quite fit?

What will you look for / research / have on hand next time?

What additional materials would be helpful for the next lesson?

And for this lesson next year?

Teacher Reflection

What is your overall impression of your experience of this lesson / module?

Module 1

It's All You

Mindful Message:
When we practice paying attention to what we feel in our bodies, we can choose wisely and take better care of ourselves.

Lesson 4 - Rest

Goal: Students practice shifting energy to settle and rest.

Materials:

- Chimes
- Paper & pencils

Pre-Practice

2-Handed Belly Breath

SEL Connection:

Recognize and create a feeling of safety.

GoNoodle Videos:

THINK ABOUT IT – *Find Peace*

THINK ABOUT IT – *Rest Well*

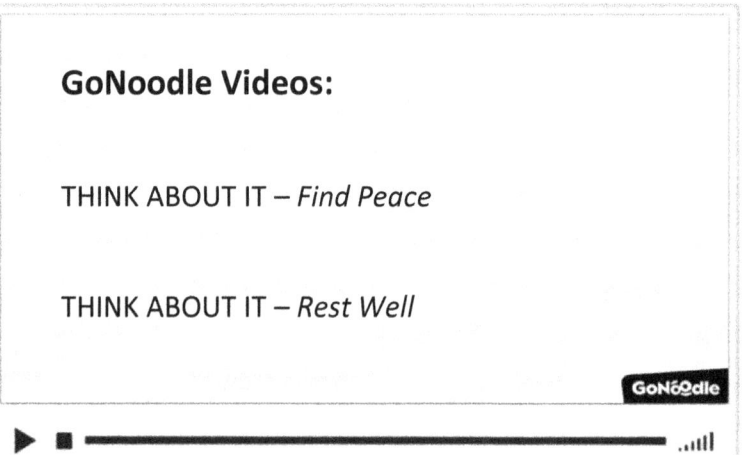

FOCUS

Engage: Video

THINK ABOUT IT- *Find Peace*

Attention: Chimes

Place your attention on the sound.

Ring Chime 1 time.

Be still for the next two sounds.

Ring chime 2 times.

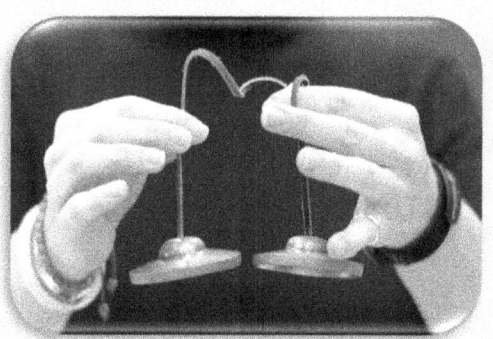

Breath: Belly Breath

Place one hand on your belly.

Model remaining still and noticing movement in the belly for two breaths.

Gently stare at a spot or close your eyes for 2 more belly breaths.

MINDFUL MOVES

We all get to move by CHOICE.
Notice how your body feels then decide how to sit and how to move.

Mindful Mountain

Put a picture of a mountain in your mind:

    a tall peak with gentle slopes,

    sitting solidly and still on the ground.

Sit tall, shoulders down, settle in, hands rest,

    muscles soften, eyes close or stare.

Be a mindful mountain.

Hand Jive*

Sit comfortably.

Wring hands as if washing them.

Slowly, then quickly.

Wiggle fingers. Open and close. Pause.

Circle closed fists. Circle open hands.

Try same directions, different

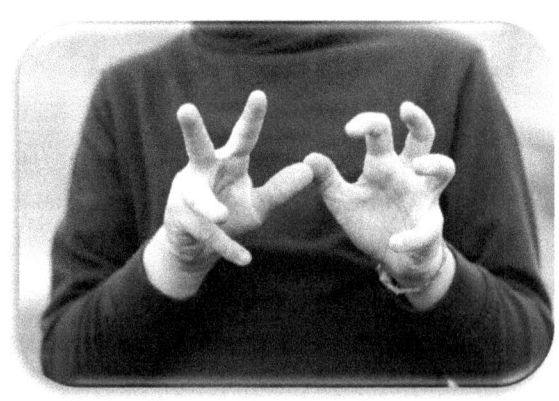

directions, quickly, slowly, and then try super-duper extra slow motion.

    * Challenge: Clasp fingers – rotate, turn inside-out and press in front, up and to sides.

Hands in lap, rest.

Mindful Circles*

Sit tall and relaxed.

Notice how it feels to circle each at your own pace.

- Shoulders
- Elbows
- Fingers **Challenge (try one at a time)**
- Big Toes

Try moving in one direction, then the other.

Rainbow Breath

Sit strong and relaxed… or stand!

Arms hang down at sides.

Breathe in to reach arms wide and up.

Pause. Breathe out while hands remain high.

Breathe in tall!

Now breathe out to float arms wide and down.

Repeat with breath two or three more times.

EXPLORE

Solo Reflection

All students need paper and pencil.

1. **Guide Statement:**

   Think of your favorite activity, from what we have done together so far in these lessons.

   Name it and describe WHY it's your favorite.

   Brainstorm a few as a group, if needed.

2. **Guide Questions:**

   Draw or write what comes to mind.

   - *What do you look like when you're taking care of yourself?*

   - *What can you do to help yourself rest OR even go to sleep?*

Reflection: Ask students for verbal reflections.

BALANCE

Bent Arrow Balance

Sit tall in a chair or on the floor.

Stare at a spot in front of you.

Lift one bent leg and hold, now add other leg.

Focus and stay steady. Breathe.

Adjust and begin again, if needed.

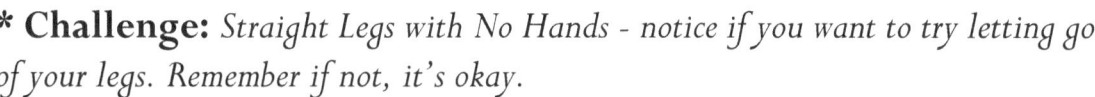

   * Challenge: *Straight Legs with No Hands - notice if you want to try letting go of your legs. Remember if not, it's okay.*

Adjust and repeat.   Another challenge? Stay for 5, 4, 3, 2, 1.

REST

Seated Plank

Lean back in your chair.

Stretch your legs long and point your toes.

Extend arms up and behind, reach.

Make your body as straight as a plank

   but remain comfortable.

Maybe yawn. In fact, try to yawn!!!

Sink in your chair.

Settle and stay for a few breaths. **Rest.**

GoNoodle Video:

THINK ABOUT IT – *Rest Well*

Lesson Reflection for Teaching Mindful Moods

Highlights

What did students report / notice?

What did you notice, for you or for students?

Components

What aspects can you repeat as a practice, beyond the lesson?

What can you change to be more relevant for your students?

What can be tied in and integrated into other subjects or themes?

Planning, Spacing & Pacing

How did the timing play a role in the experience of the lesson?

What will you adjust for next lesson or next year?

Resources & Materials

What worked well?

What didn't quite fit?

What will you look for / research / have on hand next time?

What additional materials would be helpful for the next lesson?

And for this lesson next year?

Teacher Reflection

What is your overall impression of your experience of this lesson / module?

Module 2
Name It & Tame It

Mindful Message: When we get to know our emotions, we can respect them and mindfully practice managing them.

Teaching Preparation for Module 2

LESSON GOAL	SEL CONNECTION	TEACHING TOOLS	GoNoodle VIDEOS
Lesson 1 **Name It** Students identify a range of feelings/emotions.	Recognize the universal experience of emotions and learn new ones as well.	**Materials:** Chimes **Pre-Practice:** Heart & Belly Breath	**Videos:** FLOW – *Twist & Turn* BLAZER Fresh – *Mood Walk*
Lesson 2 **Weigh It** Students distinguish between heavy and light emotions.	Understand the weight of our own and others' emotions.	**Materials:** Chimes Feather & stone Activity Sheet – *Feather and Stone* **Pre-Practice:** Heart & Belly Breath	**Videos:** FLOW – *Light as a Feather* FLOW – *Twist & Turn* FLOW – *Melting*
Lesson 3 **Feel It** Students identify where and how emotions show up in their bodies.	Normalize sensations in the body that are connected to emotions.	**Materials:** Chimes Crayons/markers Activity Sheet – *Emotional Body Map* **Pre-Practice:** Gentle Bobble Head	**Videos:** FLOW – *Melting* BLAZER Fresh – *Body Says What?*
Lesson 4 **Tame It** Students demonstrate how emotions play-out in behavior.	Together, we act out emotions safely and accept others' perceptions.	**Materials:** Chimes **Pre-Practice:** Gentle Bobble Head	**Videos:** FLOW – *Light as a Feather* BLAZER Fresh – *Mood Walk*

Wynne Kinder, M. Ed.

Teaching Components for Module 2

FOCUS	MINDFUL MOVES	EXPLORE	BALANCE & REST
Engage: Video FLOW- *Twist and Turn* **Attention:** Chimes **Breath:** Heart & Belly Breath	Mindful Mountain Bobble Head Twist and Turn Lifting Breath	**Chalk Talk:** *What do people feel or experience?* **Video:** BLAZER Fresh – *Mood Walk*	**Balance:** Heron **Rest:** Chime Breath
Engage: Video FLOW – *Light as a Feather* **Attention:** Chimes **Breath:** Heart & Belly Breath	Mindful Mountain Bobble Head Twist and Turn Lifting Breath **Video:** FLOW - *Twist & Turn*	**Think - Pair - Share:** Activity Sheet – *Feathers & Stones* **Video:** FLOW - *Melting*	**Balance:** Heron **Rest:** Chime Breath

Engage: Video FLOW - *Melting*
 	
Attention: Chimes
 	
Breath:
Heart & Belly Breath
	Mindful Mountain
	Bobble Head
	   with *Challenge
	Twist and Turn
	Lifting Breath
	   with *Challenge
		Solo Reflection:
		
		Activity Sheet - *Emotional Body Map*
		
		Video:
		BLAZER Fresh – *Body Says What?*
			Balance:
			Heron
			   with *Challenge
			
			Rest:
			Chime Breath
			   with *Challenge

Engage: Video BLAZER FRESH - *Mood Walk*
 	
Attention: Chimes
 	
Breath: Heart & Belly Breath
	Mindful Mountain
	Bobble Head
	   with *Challenge
	Twist and Turn
	Lifting Breath
	   with *Challenge
	
	Video:
	FLOW – *Light as a Feather*
		Group Activity:
		
		Charade Parade
			Balance:
			Heron with *Challenge
			
			Rest:
			Chime Breath with *Challenge

Module 2
Name It & Tame It

Mindful Message:
When we get to know and respect our own emotions, we can mindfully practice managing them.

Lesson 1 – Name It

Goal: Students identify a range of feelings/emotions.

Materials:

- Chimes

Pre-Practice

Heart & Belly Breath

SEL Connection:

Recognize the universal experience of emotions and learn new ones as well.

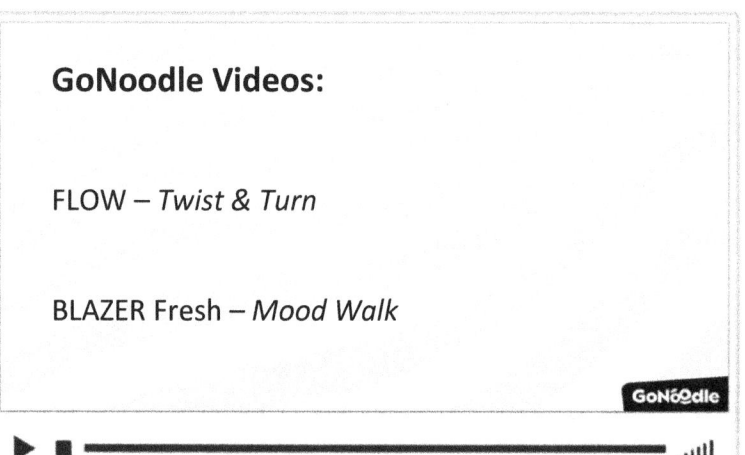

GoNoodle Videos:

FLOW – *Twist & Turn*

BLAZER Fresh – *Mood Walk*

FOCUS

Engage: Video

    FLOW- *Twist & Turn*

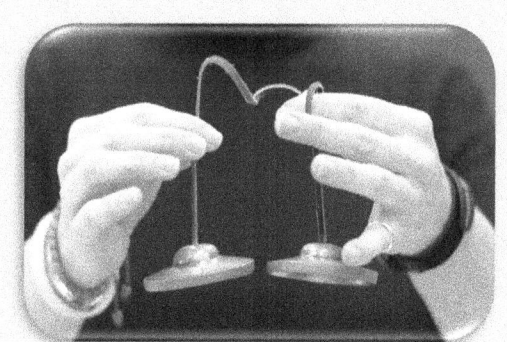

Attention: Chimes

Place your attention on the sound.

Ring Chime 1 time.

Be still for the next two sounds.

Ring chime 2 more times.

Breath: Heart & Belly Breath

Sit comfortably, like a mountain.

Place one hand on upper chest, over heart.

Place other hand on low belly.

Breathe in and out.

Notice breath moving in the body for 3 more breaths.

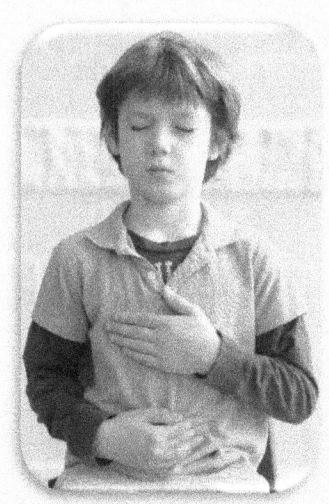

MINDFUL MOVES

**We all get to move by CHOICE.
Notice how your body feels, then decide how to move.**

Mindful Mountain

Put a picture of a mountain in your mind:

    a tall peak with gentle slopes,

    sitting solidly and still on the ground.

Sit tall, shoulders down, settle in, hands rest,

    muscles soften, eyes close or stare.

Be a mindful mountain.

Bobble Head

Sit tall without leaning.

Lift and lower the chin as much and or as little

    and as fast or as slow as you would like.

Tilt one ear down to shoulder on one side.

Return to center then try titling to the other side. Carefully tilt.

Continue tilting side to side. Slowly.

Be slow, be careful.

Try even slower.

Twist & Turn

Sit like a mountain.

Place hands on the outside of your right leg.

Breathe in to sit tall.

Breathe out to rotate shoulders to the right.

Carefully let your body twist and turn gently.

Breathe in.

Breathe out to turn a little more, if **comfortable**.

Breathe in to return to center.

Repeat to the left.

Lifting Breath

Sit tall.

Place hands palms up on legs/in lap.

Inhale slowly to raise right hand.

Pause.

Flip palm down, hand floats down
> with your slow out-breath.

Repeat with the other hand.

Continue with two more of each hand.

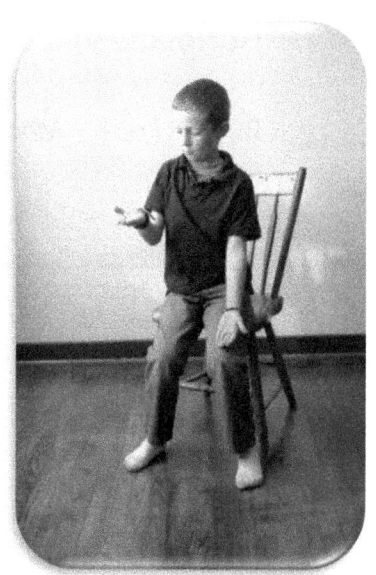

EXPLORE

Chalk Talk

Guide Questions:

What emotions do people feel? OR

What feelings do people experience?

Sample Answers: sad, angry, happy, disappointment, yucky, okay...

GoNoodle Video Options:

BLAZER Fresh – *Mood Walk*

Reflection: Ask students for verbal reflections.

BALANCE

Heron Balance

Stand tall.

Focus eyes on one spot.

Inhale to lift arms wide.

Exhale slowly, while arms remain.

Inhale to lift one knee, hip-height.

Exhale to stay steady. Breathe.

Stay for 5, 4, 3, 2, 1.

With next exhale, lower foot and arms.

Repeat on the other side.

REST

Chime Breath

Sit comfortably.

Breathe in… Breathe out slowly with sound.

Ring chime.

Repeat two more times.

Rest.

Lesson Reflection for Teaching Mindful Moods

Highlights

What did students report / notice?

What did you notice, for you or for students?

Components

What aspects can you repeat as a practice, beyond the lesson?

What can you change to be more relevant for your students?

What can be tied in and integrated into other subjects or themes?

Planning, Spacing & Pacing

How did the timing play a role in the experience of the lesson?

What will you adjust for next lesson or next year?

Resources & Materials

What worked well?

What didn't quite fit?

What will you look for / research / have on hand next time?

What additional materials would be helpful for the next lesson?

And for this lesson next year?

Teacher Reflection

What is your overall impression of your experience of this lesson / module?

Mindful Moods

| Module 2 **Name It & Tame It** | **Mindful Message:** When we get to know and respect our own emotions, we can mindfully practice managing them. |

Lesson 2 – Weigh It

Goal: Students distinguish between heavy and light emotions.

Materials:

- Chimes
- Feather & stone
- Activity Sheet – *Feathers & Stones*

Pre-Practice

Heart & Belly Breath

SEL Connection:

Understand the weight of our own and others' emotions.

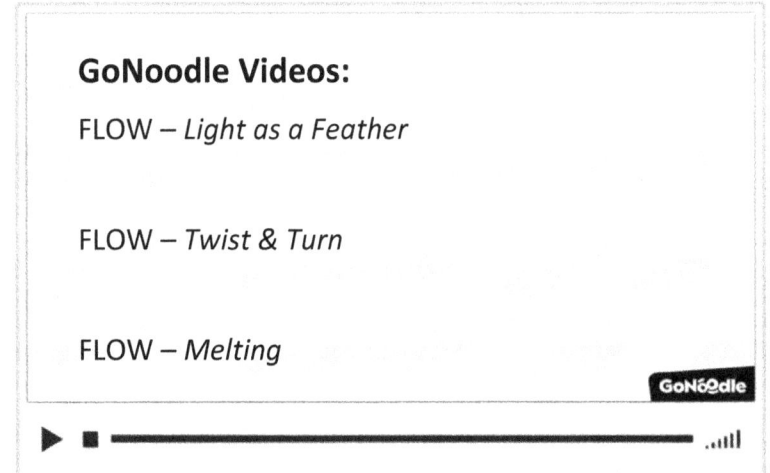

GoNoodle Videos:

FLOW – *Light as a Feather*

FLOW – *Twist & Turn*

FLOW – *Melting*

FOCUS

Engage: Video

FLOW – *Light as a Feather*

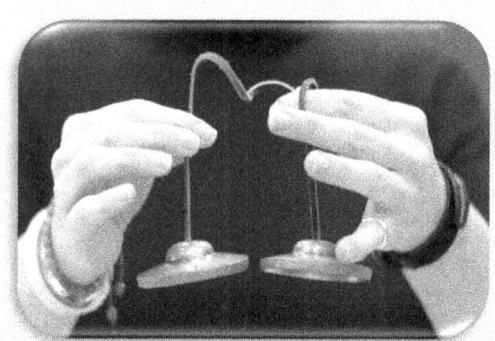

Attention: Chimes

Bring your attention to this sound.

Ring Chime 1 time.

Be still for the next two sounds.

Ring chime 2 times.

Breath: Heart & Belly Breath

Sit comfortably, tall like a mountain.

Place one hand on your upper chest, over your heart.

Place other hand on low belly.

Breathe a few times.

Notice breath moving in body for 3 breaths.

Which hand feels more movement?

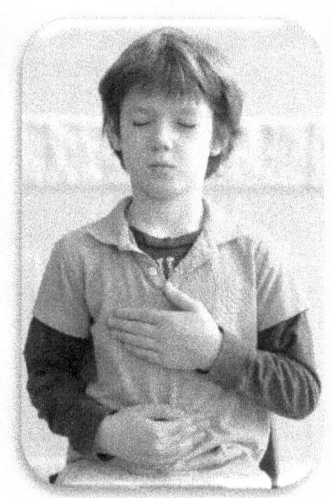

MINDFUL MOVES

**We all get to move by CHOICE.
Notice how your body feels and decide how to move.**

Mindful Mountain

Put a picture of a mountain in your mind:

    a tall peak with gentle slopes,

    sitting solidly and still on the ground.

Sit tall, shoulders down, settle in, hands rest,

    muscles soften, eyes close or stare.

Be a mindful mountain.

Bobble Head

Sit tall without leaning.

Lift and lower the chin as much and or as little

    and as fast or as slow as you would like.

Tilt one ear down to shoulder on one side.

Return to center then try titling to the other side. Carefully tilt.

Continue tilting side to side. Slowly.

Be slow, be careful.

Try even slower.

Which direction feel best to you? Up and down or tilting side to side?

Twist & Turn

Sit like a mountain.

Place hands on the outside of your right leg.

Breathe in to sit tall.

Breathe out to rotate shoulders to the right.

Carefully let your body twist and turn gently.

Breathe in.

Breathe out to turn a little more, if **comfortable**.

Breathe in to return to center.

Repeat to the left.

GoNoodle Video Options:

FLOW – *Twist & Turn*

Lifting Breath

Sit tall.

Place hands palms up on legs/in lap.

Inhale slowly to raise right hand.

Pause.

Flip palm down, hand floats down with outbreath.

Repeat with left hand.

Continue with two more of each hand.

Take your time and try by yourself.

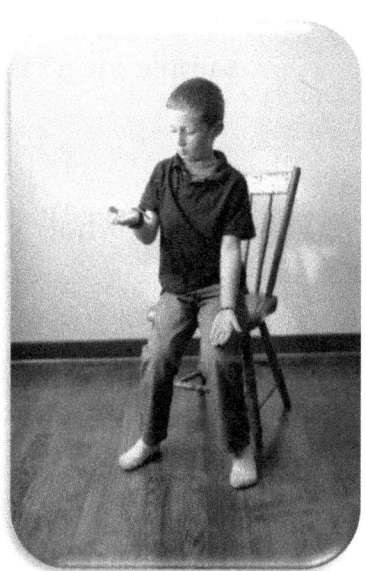

EXPLORE

Think - Pair - Share

Activity Sheet - *Feathers & Stones*

THINK *of emotions that might be <u>heavy</u> or hard to handle.*

THINK *of emotions that are <u>light</u> and easy to feel.*

In PAIRS, write light emotions in the feathers.

    Sample answers: love, excitement, funniness...

Write heavy emotions in the stones.

    Sample ideas: impatience, just yucky, sad, mad...

SHARE with whole group. Comparisons, contrasts...

GoNoodle Video Options:

FLOW - *Melting*

BALANCE

Heron Balance

Stand tall.

Focus eyes on one spot.

Inhale to lift arms wide.

Exhale slowly while arms remain.

Inhale to lift one knee, hip-height.

Exhale to stay steady. Keep breathing and focusing.

Stay for 5, 4, 3, 2, 1.

Exhale to lower both foot and arms.

Repeat on other side.

REST

Chime Breath

Sit comfortably.

Breathe in… Breathe out slowly with sound.

Ring chime…

Repeat two more times.

Rest.

Lesson Reflection for Teaching Mindful Moods

Highlights

What did students report / notice?

What did you notice, for you or for students?

Components

What aspects can you repeat as a practice, beyond the lesson?

What can you change to be more relevant for your students?

What can be tied in and integrated into other subjects or themes?

Planning, Spacing & Pacing

How did the timing play a role in the experience of the lesson?

What will you adjust for next lesson or next year?

Resources & Materials

What worked well?

What didn't quite fit?

What will you look for / research / have on hand next time?

What additional materials would be helpful for the next lesson?

And for this lesson next year?

Teacher Reflection

What is your overall impression of your experience of this lesson / module?

Module 2
Name It & Tame It

Mindful Message:
When we get to know and respect our own emotions, we can mindfully practice managing them.

Lesson 3 – Feel It

Goal: Students identify where and how emotions show up in their bodies.

Materials:

- Chimes
- Crayons/markers
- Activity Sheet – *Emotional Body Map*

Pre-Practice

Gentle Bobble Head

SEL Connection:

Normalize sensations in the body that are connected to emotions.

GoNoodle Videos:

FLOW – *Melting*

BLAZER Fresh – *Body Says What?*

FOCUS

Engage: Video

FLOW — *Melting*

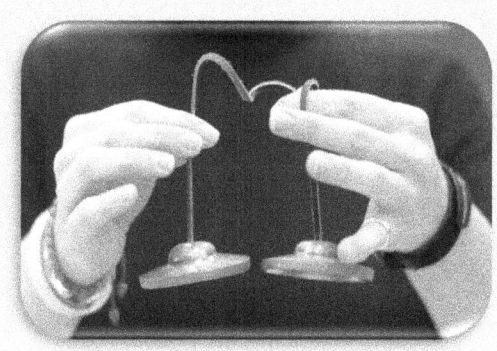

Attention: Chimes

Bring your attention to the sound.

Ring Chime 1 time.

Be still and quiet for the next two sounds.

Ring chime 2 times.

Breath: Heart & Belly Breath

Sit comfortably, at ease, like a mountain.

Place one hand on your upper chest, just over your heart.

Place the other hand on your lower belly.

Notice breath moving in the body for 3 breaths.

Switch hands. Breathe.

Any difference?

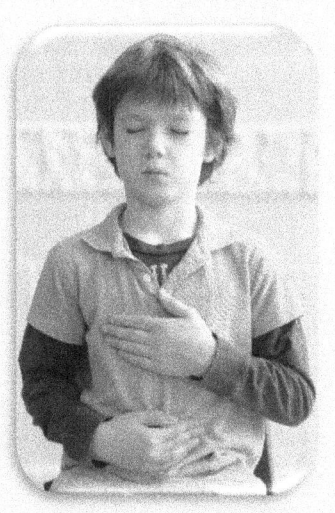

MINDFUL MOVES

**We all get to move by CHOICE.
Notice how your body feels. Sit how you choose. Move how you choose.**

Mindful Mountain

Put a picture of a mountain in your mind:

    a tall peak with gentle slopes,

    sitting solidly and still on the ground.

Sit tall, shoulders down, settle in, hands rest,

    muscles soften, eyes close or stare down.

Be a mindful mountain.

Bobble Head*

Sit tall, without leaning.

Lift and lower chin as much or as little

    as you wish. Go slowly.

Pause when you feel done.

Now tilt one ear down to the shoulder on one side,

    and then return to center and tilt the other ear on the other side.

Go side to side a few more times.

* Challenge: Gently and slowly turn your head side to side.

Be slow, be careful.

Twist & Turn

Sit like a mountain.

Place hands on the outside of your right leg.

Breathe in to sit tall.

Breathe out to rotate shoulders to the right.

Carefully let your body twist and turn gently.

Breathe in.

Breathe out to turn a little more, if **comfortable**.

Breathe in to return to center.

Repeat to the left. Then try each side again.

Lifting Breath*

Sit tall.

Place hands palms up on legs/in lap.

Inhale slowly to raise your right hand.

Flip palm down, hand floats down with outbreath.

Repeat with left hand.

Continue with two more of each hand.

* Challenge: Lift both hands with the same breath.

Flip and breathe out to float down.

Repeat with breath two more times.

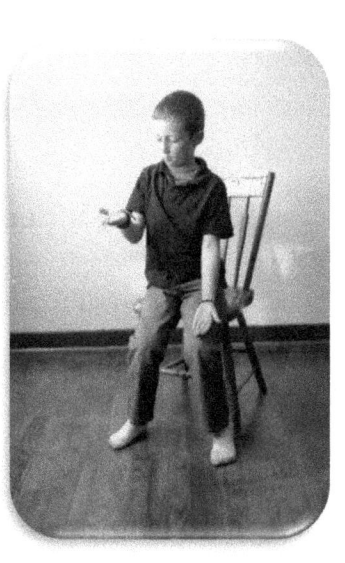

EXPLORE

Solo Reflection:

Activity Sheet - *Emotional Body Map*

1. **Guide Question:** *How does your BELLY feel when you are worried?*

    Write or Draw that on your sheet.

2. **Guide Question:** *How does your HEART feel when you are sad?*

    Write or Draw that on your sheet.

Extend the activity, write on board:

   Joyful Mouth …

   Angry Hands …

   Happy Eyes …

———————

GoNoodle Video:

BLAZER Fresh – *Body Says What?*

Reflection: Ask students for verbal reflections.

BALANCE

Heron Balance*

Stand tall.

Focus eyes on one spot.

Inhale to lift arms wide. Remain to exhale slowly.

Inhale to lift one knee, hip-height.

Exhale to stay steady.

    * Challenge: Raise arms to reach tall.

Exhale to lower foot and arms.

Repeat on other side.

REST

Chime Breath*

Sit comfortably.

Breathe in… Breathe out quietly with the sound.

Ring chime…

Repeat two more times.

    * Challenge: say "Shh" with sound.

Rest.

Lesson Reflection for Teaching Mindful Moods

Highlights

What did students report / notice?

What did you notice, for you or for students?

Components

What aspects can you repeat as a practice, beyond the lesson?

What can you change to be more relevant for your students?

What can be tied in and integrated into other subjects or themes?

Planning, Spacing & Pacing

How did the timing play a role in the experience of the lesson?

What will you adjust for next lesson or next year?

Resources & Materials

What worked well?

What didn't quite fit?

What will you look for / research / have on hand next time?

What additional materials would be helpful for the next lesson?

And for this lesson next year?

Teacher Reflection

What is your overall impression of your experience of this lesson / module?

Module 2 **Name It & Tame It**	**Mindful Message:** When we get to know and respect our own emotions, we can mindfully practice managing them.

Lesson 4 – Tame It

Goal: Students demonstrate how emotions play-out in behavior.

Materials:

- Chimes

Pre-Practice

Gentle Bobble Head

SEL Connection:

Together, we act out emotions safely and accept others' perceptions.

GoNoodle Video Options:

BLAZER Fresh – *Mood Walk*

FLOW - *Light as a Feather (look for Spanish language version as well)*

Wynne Kinder, M. Ed.

FOCUS

Engage: Video

BLAZER Fresh – *Mood Walk*

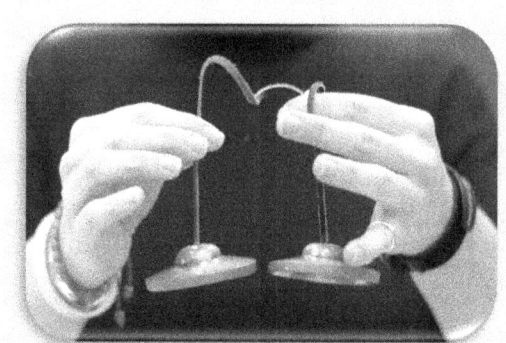

Attention: Chimes

Place your attention on the sound.

Ring Chime 1 time.

Be still for the next three sounds.

Ring chime 3 times.

Breath: Heart & Belly Breath

Sit comfortably, like a mountain.

Place one hand on your upper chest, over your heart.

Place other hand on your lower belly.

Breathe.

Notice breath moving in the core of your body.

Eyes might close or look down for 3 more breaths.

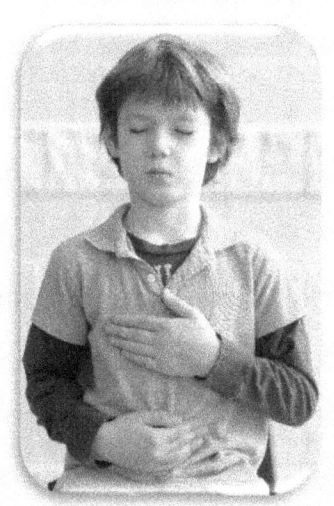

MINDFUL MOVES

We all get to move by CHOICE.
Notice how your body feels. Sit so you feel at ease, but ready to move.

Mindful Mountain

Put a picture of a mountain in your mind:

    a tall peak with gentle slopes,

    sitting solidly and still on the ground.

Sit tall, shoulders down, settle in, hands rest,

    muscles soften, eyes close or stare.

Be a mindful mountain.

Bobble Head*

Sit tall without leaning back or forward.

Lift and lower chin a few times.

Return to center.

Tilt one ear down to the shoulder on one side.

Return to center. Try the other side. Keep tilting side to side for a few more.

Return to center. Gently and slowly turn head side to side. Maybe a few more times.

* Challenge: Pick what you like to do most in Bobble Head, do that for a bit.

Be slow, be careful.

Twist & Turn

Sit like a mountain.

Place hands on the outside of your right leg.

Breathe in to sit tall.

Breathe out to rotate shoulders to the right.

Carefully let your body twist and turn gently.

Breathe in.

Breathe out to turn a little more, if **comfortable**.

Breathe in to return to center. Repeat to the left.

Notice how each side feels. Rest for a moment.

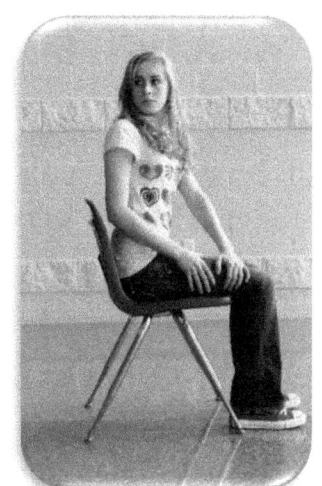

Lifting Breath*

Sit tall.

Place hands palms up on legs/in lap.

Inhale slowly to raise right hand.

Flip palm down, hand floats with outbreath.

Repeat with left hand.

Continue with two more of each hand.

* **Challenge:** Lift both hands with the same breath. Breathe out to float both down.

Repeat with breath, two more times.

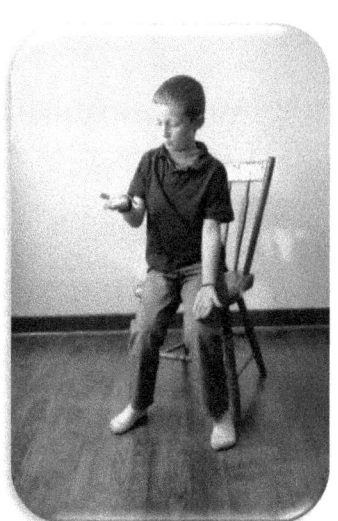

GoNoodle Video:

FLOW – *Light as a Feather*

EXPLORE

Group Activity:

Charade Parade

We can claim and tame our emotions.

Students form a large circle. They will want to remain quiet to hear the directions.

Students begin moving in the same direction:

1. Marching Mad
2. Joyful Jump
3. Slowly Sad
4. Walking Worried
5. Hop Happy
6. Stop Scared, Gleeful Go, Stop Scared, Gleeful Go…
7. Hopeful Halt
8. _____

Repeat in different order?

GoNoodle Video:

BLAZER Fresh – *Mood Walk*

BALANCE

Heron Balance*

Stand tall.

Focus eyes on one spot.

Inhale to lift arms wide.

Exhale slowly.

Inhale to lift one knee, hip-height.

Exhale to stay steady.

    ***Challenge:** Raise arms to reach tall.

Exhale to lower foot and arms.

Repeat on other side.

REST

Chime Breath*

Sit comfortably.

Breathe in… Breathe out slowly with sound.

Ring chime…

Repeat two more times.

    ***Challenge:** Buzz like a bee with the sound.

Rest.

Lesson Reflection for Teaching Mindful Moods

Highlights

What did students report / notice?

What did you notice, for you or for students?

Components

What aspects can you repeat as a practice, beyond the lesson?

What can you change to be more relevant for your students?

What can be tied in and integrated into other subjects or themes?

Planning, Spacing & Pacing

How did the timing play a role in the experience of the lesson?

What will you adjust for next lesson or next year?

Resources & Materials

What worked well?

What didn't quite fit?

What will you look for / research / have on hand next time?

What additional materials would be helpful for the next lesson?

And for this lesson next year?

Teacher Reflection

What is your overall impression of your experience of this lesson / module?

Module 3
Helpful Emotions

Mindful Message: When we are mindful of how our emotions affect us, we can let them guide us – not drive us.

Teaching Preparation for Module 3

LESSON & GOAL	SEL CONNECTION	TEACHING TOOLS	GoNoodle VIDEOS
Lesson 1 **Emotions Speak** Students recognize the helpfulness of their emotions.	Emotions tell us so much about ourselves and about what others might be feeling as well.	**Materials:** Chimes **Pre-Practice:** Gentle Twist & Turn	**Videos:** FLOW – *Bring it Down* BLAZER FRESH – *Emotions Grow & Shrink*
Lesson 2 **Angry Fists** Students recognize the value of anger and are confident that they can handle it.	Explore the nature of anger, in ourselves and in others.	**Materials:** Chimes Index cards & pencils Mr. Rogers' Poem/Song *What Do You Do?* **Pre-Practice:** Gentle Hand Jive	**Videos:** FLOW – *Switch* FLOW – *Let's Unwind*
Lesson 3 **Worried Belly** Students learn to manage worry with awareness, attention, and movement.	Consider *Worry Clouds* and other strategies as helpful self-care tools.	**Materials:** Chimes Pencils/crayons Activity Sheet – *Worry Clouds* **Pre-Practice:** Attention to Feet on Floor	**Videos:** THINK ABOUT IT – *Let It Go* BLAZER FRESH – *Emotions Grow & Shrink*
Lesson 4 **Knots of Emotions** Students recognize that even knotted emotions are manageable.	Untie knotted emotions (and bodies), together.	**Materials:** Chimes Emotion String **Pre-Practice:** Gentle Hand Jive	**Videos:** FLOW – *Swirling* THINK ABOUT IT – *Be a Team Player*

Teaching Components for Module 3

FOCUS	MINDFUL MOVES	EXPLORE	BALANCE & REST

Engage: Video
 	
FLOW –
Bring it Down
 	
Attention: Chimes
 	
Breath: Rib Breath
	Mindful Mountain
	Hand Jive
	    with *Challenge
	Press & Let Go
	Elevator Breath
		Chalk Talk:
		
		Emotions tell you so much - about you and what you need.
		
		Video:
		BLAZER FRESH –
		Emotions grow & Shrink
			Balance:
			Tree
			
			Rest:
			Chime Breath
			    with *Challenge

Engage: Video
 	
FLOW - *Switch*
 	
Attention: Chimes
 	
Breath: Rib Breath
	Mindful Mountain
	Hand Jive
	    with *Challenge
	Press & Let Go
	Elevator Breath
		Group Activity:
		
		What Do You Do? (with The Mad that You Feel)
		by Mister Rogers
		
		Video:
		FLOW - *Let's Unwind*
			Balance:
			One of Each
			
			Rest:
			Chime Breath
			    with *Challenge

Engage: Video
 	
THINK ABOUT IT –
Let it Go
 	
Attention: Chimes
 	
Breath: Rib Breath
	Mindful Mountain
	Hand Jive
	    with *Challenge
	Washing Machine
	Elevator Breath
	    with *Challenge
		Solo Reflection:
		
		Activity Sheet –
		Worry Clouds
		
		Video:
		BLAZER FRESH –
		Emotions Grow & Shrink
			Balance:
			Tree
			
			Rest:
			Chime Breath
			    with *Challenge

Engage: Video
 	
FLOW - *Swirling*
 	
Attention: Chimes
 	
Breath: Rib Breath
	Mindful Mountain
	Hand Jive
	    with *Challenge
	Washing Machine
	Elevator Breath
	    with *Challenge
		Group Activity:
		
		Begin with Video:
		THINK ABOUT IT -
		Be a Team Player
		
		Human Knot:
		Work and play in teams
			Balance:
			One of Each
			    with *Challenge
			
			Attention Returns:
			Resting Hill

Module 3 **Helpful Emotions**	**Mindful Message:** When we are mindful of how our emotions affect us, we can let them guide us – not drive us.

Lesson 1 – Emotions Speak

Goal: Students recognize the helpfulness of their emotions.

Materials:

- Chimes

Pre-Practice: Gentle Twist & Turn

SEL Connection:

Emotions tell us so much about ourselves and about what others might be feeling as well.

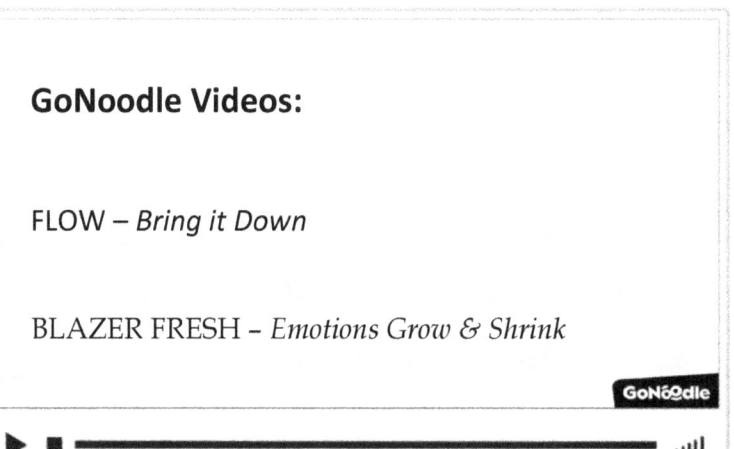

GoNoodle Videos:

FLOW – *Bring it Down*

BLAZER FRESH – *Emotions Grow & Shrink*

FOCUS

Engage: Video

FLOW – *Bring it Down*

Attention: Chimes

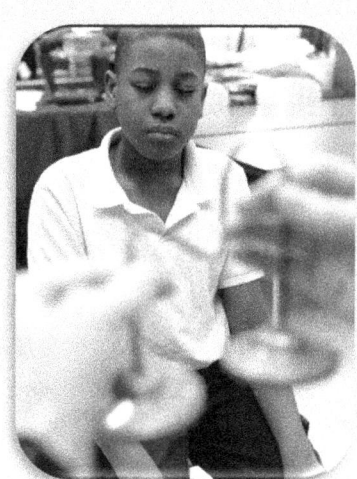

Direct your attention to the sound.

Ring Chime 1 time.

Be still for the next three sounds.

Allow for longer pauses between.

Ring chime 3 times.

Breath: Rib Breath

Sit tall with shoulders down and back. Feel at ease.

Place hands on front, sides, or back of your rib cage.

Notice subtle movement while breathing in and out.

Continue for three breath cycles.

Ask students to reflect on what they felt.

MINDFUL MOVES

We all get to move by CHOICE.
Notice how your body feels and decide how to move.

Mindful Mountain

Put a picture of a mountain in your mind:

    a tall peak with gentle slopes,

    sitting solidly and still on the ground.

Sit tall, shoulders down, settle in, hands rest,

    muscles soften, eyes close or stare.

Be a mindful mountain. *Remain for ~30 seconds, a student count down.

Hand Jive*

Sit comfortably.

Wring hands as if washing them.

Slowly, then quickly.

Wiggle fingers. Open and close. Pause.

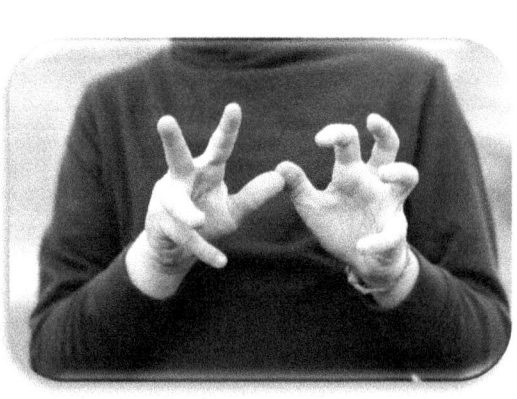

Circle closed fists. Circle open hands.

Shake them, a little more. Pause.

* Challenge: Clasp fingers – rotate, turn inside-out and press in front, up and to sides.

With one arm extended and palm up, use opposite hand to **gently** push fingers down to stretch palm and wrist. Repeat with other hand.

Hands in lap, rest.

Press and Let Go

Mindful mountains sit tall.

Breathe in to press hands **forward**,

    with arms flat.

Breathe out to return arms and hands to sides,

    let go.

Breathe in to press **up**.

Breathe out to return, let go

Breathe in to press **behind** (fingers down).

Breathe out to return, let go.

Breathe in to press to each side, **wide**.

Breathe out to let go.

Repeat.

Elevator Breath

Sit like a mindful mountain with shoulders down.

Place hands palm to palm, flat in front of your

    belly button.

Lift top (elevator) hand with inhale to top of head.

Exhale to float elevator hand down to rest on the other (ground floor) hand.

Repeat 2 times.

Then switch hands if you wish. Repeat 2 more times.

EXPLORE

Chalk Talk:

Teacher writes on the board:

- Sadness tells you…
- Love tells you…
- Worry tells you…
- Anger tells you…
- _____
- _____

Sample Ideas:

- *Sadness…that you lost something / you need help*
- *Love…that you are cared for / have others in life*
- *Worry…that it's time to fix something / check on something*
- *Anger…that something isn't right / that you need to act*

GoNoodle Video Options:

BLAZER FRESH – *Emotions Grow & Shrink*

Reflection: Ask students for verbal reflections.

BALANCE

Tree Balance

Stand strong.

Focus eyes on one spot.

Inhale to lift arms wide and high.

Exhale to be still.

Inhale to lift one foot and place on other leg.

Exhale to stay steady. Breathe naturally.

Be a strong tree for 5, 4, 3, 2, 1.

Inhale grow tall and reach.

Exhale to lower foot and arms slowly and together.

Repeat with other leg.

REST

Chime Breath*

Sit comfortably.

Breathe in… pause… Ring chime…

Breathe out slowly with sound.

*** Challenge**: For the next 2 chimes,

hum with the sound.

Rest.

Lesson Reflection for Teaching Mindful Moods

Highlights

What did students report / notice?

What did you notice, for you or for students?

Components

What aspects can you repeat as a practice, beyond the lesson?

What can you change to be more relevant for your students?

What can be tied in and integrated into other subjects or themes?

Planning, Spacing & Pacing

How did the timing play a role in the experience of the lesson?

What will you adjust for next lesson or next year?

Resources & Materials

What worked well?

What didn't quite fit?

What will you look for / research / have on hand next time?

What additional materials would be helpful for the next lesson?

And for this lesson next year?

Teacher Reflection

What is your overall impression of your experience of this lesson / module?

Module 3 **Helpful Emotions**	**Mindful Message:** When we are mindful of how our emotions affect us, we can let them guide us – not drive us.

Lesson 2 – Angry Fists

Goal: Students recognize the value of anger and are confident that they can handle it.

Pre-Practice:

Gentle Hand Jive

Materials:

- Chimes
- Index cards & pencils
- Mr. Rogers Poem/Song: *What Do You Do?*
  www.neighborhoodarchive.com/music/songs/what_do_you_do.html

SEL Connection:

Explore the nature of anger in ourselves and in others.

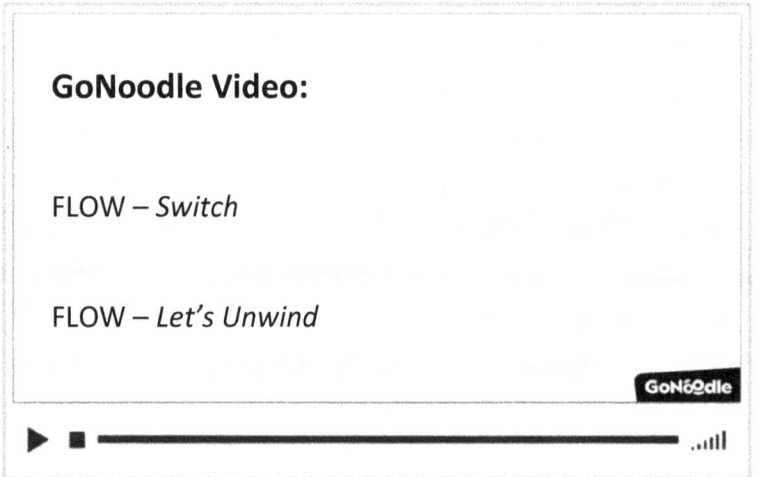

GoNoodle Video:

FLOW – *Switch*

FLOW – *Let's Unwind*

FOCUS

Engage: Video

FLOW – *Switch*

Attention: Chimes

Place your attention on the sound.

Ring Chime 1 time.

Be still for the next two sounds.

Ring chime 2 times.

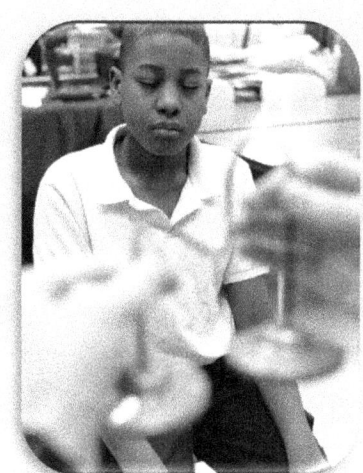

Breath: Rib Breath

Sit tall with shoulders down and back.

Place hands on front, side, or back of your rib cage.

Notice subtle movement while breathing in and out.

Repeat for 3 breath cycles.

Reflect: Where do you notice breath most? Sides, front or back?

MINDFUL MOVES

**We all get to move by CHOICE.
Notice how your body feels and decide how to move.**

Mindful Mountain

Put a picture of a mountain in your mind:

    a tall peak with gentle slopes,

    sitting solidly and still on the ground.

Sit tall, shoulders down, settle in, hands rest,

    muscles soften, eyes close or stare.

Be a mindful mountain. Be a breathing mountain.

Hand Jive*

Sit comfortably.

Wring hands as if washing them.

Slowly, then quickly.

Wiggle fingers. Open and close. Pause.

Circle closed fists. Circle open hands.

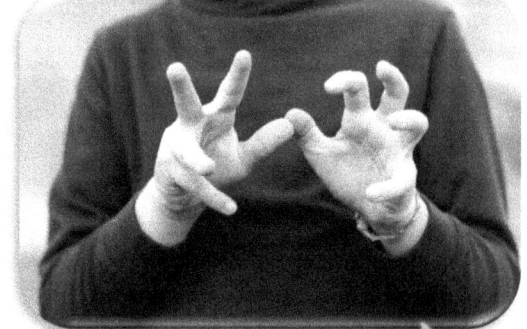

* Challenge: Clasp fingers – rotate, turn inside-out and press in front, up and to sides.

With one arm extended and palm up, use opposite hand to **gently** press fingers down to stretch palm and wrist. Repeat with other hand.

Place hands in lap to rest.

Press and Let Go

Mindful mountains sit tall.

Breathe in to press hands **forward**, arms are flat like the floor.

Breathe out to return arms and hands to sides, let go. Pause and then continue.

Breathe in to press **up**.

Breathe out to return, let go

Breathe in to press **behind** (fingers down).

Breathe out to return, let go.

Breathe in to press to each side, **wide**.

Breathe out to let go. Repeat sequence 2 more times.

Elevator Breath

Sit like a mindful mountain with shoulders down.

Place hands palm to palm, flat in front of your belly button.

Lift top (elevator) hand with inhale to near top of head.

Exhale to float elevator hand down to rest on the other hand.

Repeat two times.

Then switch hands if you wish. Maybe reach higher and breathe bigger.

EXPLORE

Group Activity:

Poem/Song - *What Do You Do?* by Mister Rogers

www.neighborhoodarchive.com/music/songs/what_do_you_do.html

Guide Question:

What do you do with the mad that you feel?

Students generate lists of **what they do with the mad they feel.**

Write ideas on index card.

Teacher reads poem.

Students take a moment to add to their lists.

Guide Statement and Question:

On the back of your card, briefly describe a time when you were mad.

What did you do OR wish you had done to manage it well?
Share reflections.

BALANCE

One of Each Balance

Stand tall. Be a mountain.

Stare at a spot. Focus. Breathe.

Fold forward with slightly bent knees.

Place both hands on the floor. Be steady.

Lift one bent leg behind you. Stay focused.

Breathe.

* Challenge: Lift same-as-lifted-leg arm to reach high.

Adjust and begin again, if needed. Breathe to stay steady.

Stay for 5, 4, 3, 2, 1. When you exhale, slowly return to Standing Mountain.

Repeat (step by step) with other leg.

REST

Chime Breath*

Sit comfortably.

Breathe in… pause… Ring chime…

Breathe out slowly with sound.

* Challenge: For the next 2 chimes,

hum softly with the sound.

Rest.

Lesson Reflection for Teaching Mindful Moods

Highlights

What did students report / notice?

What did you notice, for you or for students?

Components

What aspects can you repeat as a practice, beyond the lesson?

What can you change to be more relevant for your students?

What can be tied in and integrated into other subjects or themes?

Planning, Spacing & Pacing

How did the timing play a role in the experience of the lesson?

What will you adjust for next lesson or next year?

Resources & Materials

What worked well?

What didn't quite fit?

What will you look for / research / have on hand next time?

What additional materials would be helpful for the next lesson?

And for this lesson next year?

Teacher Reflection

What is your overall impression of your experience of this lesson / module?

| Module 3 **Helpful Emotions** | **Mindful Message:** When we are mindful of how our emotions affect us, we can let them guide us – not drive us. |

Lesson 3 – Worried Belly

Goal: Students learn to manage worry with awareness, attention, and movement.

Materials:

- Chimes
- Pencils/crayons
- Activity Sheet – *Worry Clouds*

Pre-Practice:

Attention to Feet on Floor

SEL Connection:

Consider *Worry Clouds* and other strategies as helpful self-care tools.

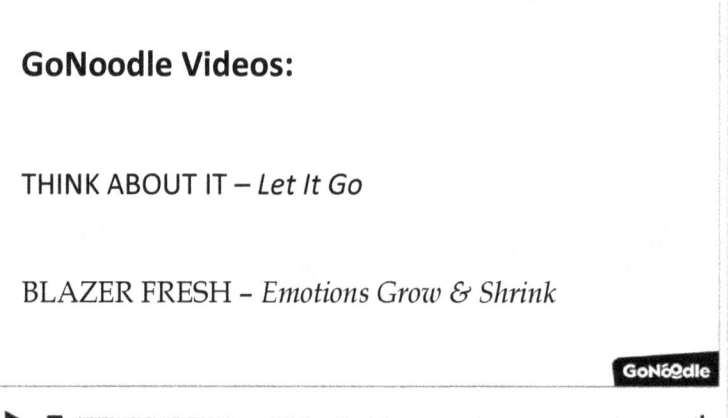

GoNoodle Videos:

THINK ABOUT IT – *Let It Go*

BLAZER FRESH – *Emotions Grow & Shrink*

FOCUS

Engage: Video

THINK ABOUT IT – *Let It Go*

Attention: Chimes

Place your attention on the sound.

Ring Chime 1 time.

Be still for the next three sounds.

Ring chime 3 more times.

Consider longer pauses between.

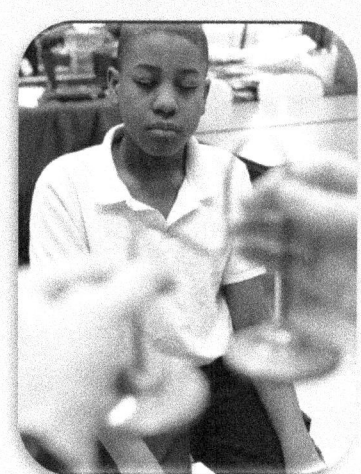

Breath: Rib Breath

Sit tall with shoulders down and back.

Place hands on front, side, or back of your rib cage.

Notice subtle movement while breathing in and out.

Repeat for 3 breath cycles.

Ask for reflections, subtle noticings.

MINDFUL MOVES

**We all get to move by CHOICE.
Notice how your body feels and decide how to move.**

Mindful Mountain

Put a picture of a mountain in your mind:

    a tall peak with gentle slopes,

    sitting solidly and still on the ground.

Sit tall, shoulders down, settle in, hands rest,

    muscles soften, eyes close or stare.

Be a mindful mountain. Remain for a minute or so.

Hand Jive*

Sit comfortably.

Wring hands as if washing them.

Slowly, then quickly.

Wiggle fingers. Open and close. Pause.

Circle closed fists. Circle open hands.

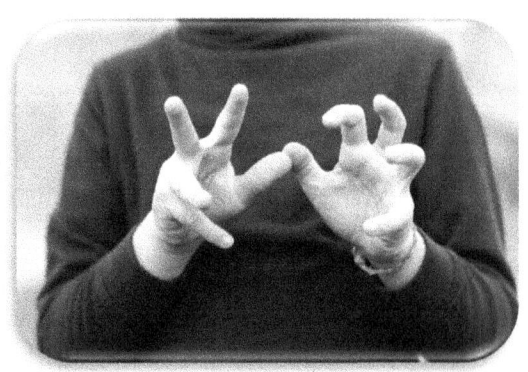

* Challenge: Clasp fingers – rotate, turn inside-out and press in front, up and to sides.

With one arm extended and palm up, use opposite hand to gentle push fingers down to stretch palm and wrist. Repeat with other hand.

Ask for other ideas of ways to creatively move hands and possibly release tension.

Washing Machine

Same beginning as twist and turn but then…

Elbows are up to the sides and fingertips are resting on shoulders.

Possibly rotate back and forth (side to side) very slowly at first.

Then if you wish, try a *little* faster. No need to match with breath.

You be the judge of what your body does.

Be safe and have fun with it.

Elevator Breath*

Sit like a mindful mountain with shoulders down.

Place hands palm to palm, flat in front of your belly button.

Lift top (elevator) hand with inhale to top of head.

Exhale to float elevator hand down to rest on the other hand.

Switch hands if you wish.

* Challenge: Try counting - 0 to 4 as elevator rises.

Count down from 4 to 0 as elevator descends.

EXPLORE

Solo Reflection:

Activity Sheet - *Worry Clouds*

Students write worries on clouds in pencil.

Use blue crayons to color sky.

Then carefully color clouds blue as well and watch worries fade.

Share by choice.

GoNoodle Video Options:

BLAZER FRESH – *Emotions Grow & Shrink*

BALANCE

Tree Balance*

Stand strong. Focus eyes on one spot.

Inhale to lift arms wide and then high.

Exhale to be still.

Inhale to lift one foot and place on other leg.

Exhale to stay steady.

> *** Challenge:** Breathe smoothly and sway with imaginary wind.
>
> Slowly lower foot and arms together.
>
> Repeat with other leg.

REST

Chime Breath*

Sit comfortably.

Breathe in… pause… *Ring chime…*

Breathe out slowly with this sound.

* **Challenge**: For the next two chimes, **sigh** with the sound.

Be quiet and still to **Rest**.

Lesson Reflection for Teaching Mindful Moods

Highlights

What did students report / notice?

What did you notice, for you or for students?

Components

What aspects can you repeat as a practice, beyond the lesson?

What can you change to be more relevant for your students?

What can be tied in and integrated into other subjects or themes?

Planning, Spacing & Pacing

How did the timing play a role in the experience of the lesson?

What will you adjust for next lesson or next year?

Resources & Materials

What worked well?

What didn't quite fit?

What will you look for / research / have on hand next time?

What additional materials would be helpful for the next lesson?

And for this lesson next year?

Teacher Reflection

What is your overall impression of your experience of this lesson / module?

| Module 3 **Helpful Emotions** | **Mindful Message:** When we are mindful of how our emotions affect us, we can let them guide us – not drive us. |

Lesson 4 – Knots of Emotions

Goal: Students recognize that even knotted emotions are manageable.

Pre-Practice:

Gentle Hand Jive

Materials:

- Chimes
- Emotion String

SEL Connection:

Untie knotted emotions (and bodies), together.

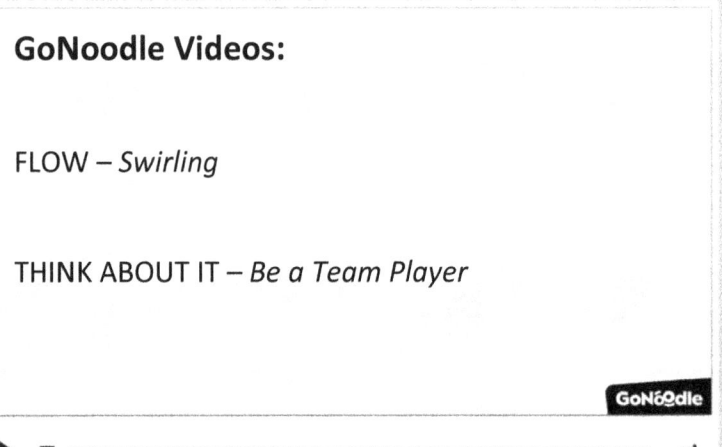

GoNoodle Videos:

FLOW – *Swirling*

THINK ABOUT IT – *Be a Team Player*

FOCUS

Engage: Video option

FLOW – *Swirling*

Attention: Chimes

Place your attention on the sound.

Ring Chime 1 time.

Be still for the next two sounds.

Ring chime 2 times.

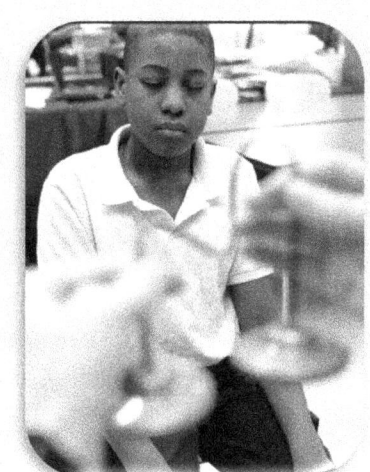

Breath: Rib Breath

Sit tall with shoulders down and back.

Place hands on front, side, or back of each rib cage.

Notice subtle movement while breathing in and out.

Repeat for three breath cycles.

Try placing one hand on front of ribs and one hand behind, on back.

Notice what happens.

MINDFUL MOVES

**We all get to move by CHOICE.
Notice how your body feels and decide how to move.**

Mindful Mountain

Put a picture of a mountain in your mind:

    a tall peak with gentle slopes,

    sitting solidly and still on the ground.

Sit tall, shoulders down, settle in, hands rest,

    muscles soften, eyes close or stare.

Be a mindful mountain.

Hand Jive*

Sit comfortably.

Wring hands as if washing them.

Slowly, then quickly.

Wiggle fingers. Open and close. Pause.

Circle closed fists. Circle open hands.

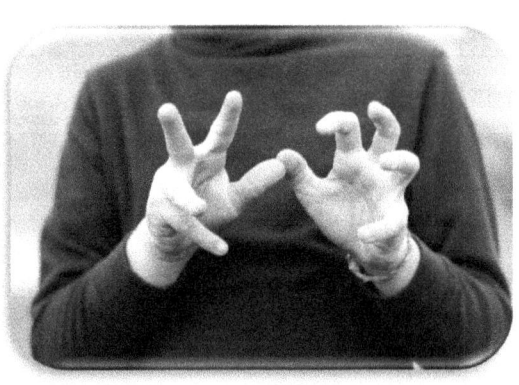

* Challenge: Clasp fingers – rotate, turn inside-out and press in front, up and arch to one side, then to the other.

With arm extended and palm up, use opposite hand to gentle push fingers down to stretch palm and wrist. Repeat with other hand.

Hands in lap, rest.

Washing Machine

Same beginning as twist and turn but then…

Elbows are up to the sides and fingertips are resting on shoulders.

Possibly rotate back and forth very slowly at first.

Then if you wish, try a little faster. No need to match with breath.

You be the judge of what your body does.

Be safe and have fun with it.

Elevator Breath*

Sit like a mindful mountain with shoulders down.

Place hands palm to palm, flat in front of your belly button.

Lift top (elevator) hand with inhale to top of head.

Exhale to float elevator hand down to rest on the other hand.

Switch hands if you wish.

*** Challenge:** Try counting 0 to 4 as elevator rises.

Super Slow Version:

Count down from 4 to 0 as elevator descends.

EXPLORE

Group Activity:

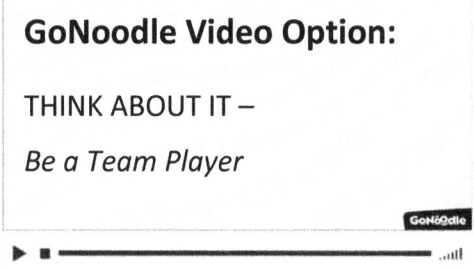

GoNoodle Video Option:

THINK ABOUT IT –
Be a Team Player

Human Knot (with string)

Our emotions can feel like they are **tying us up, like knots in this string**. But we can notice that and practice loosening those knots, with mindful moves and practices. We may do okay at this alone, but sometimes friends can help.

Here is a fun way to untie knots with others.

> In groups of 4 or 5, create a circle, facing in.
>
> Clasp hands with two people across from you, not next to you.
>
> Notice that it feels a little unsolvable at first, that's how knots are.

Talk quietly to work it out.

Untie without letting go of each other's hands.

> Experiment with larger groups if possible.

Reflect on knotted emotions and the need for others to help in the untying process sometimes.

BALANCE

One of Each Balance*

Stand tall. Be a mountain.

Stare at a spot. Focus. Breathe.

Fold forward with slightly bent knees.

Place both hands on the floor. Be steady.

Lift one bent leg behind you. Stay focused.

Breathe.

> ***Challenge?** Lift same-as-lifted-leg arm to reach high.

Adjust and begin again, if needed.

Stay for 5, 4, 3, 2, 1. Exhale to be in control as you return to Mountain.

Repeat (step by step) with other leg.

REST

Resting Hill

Rest back in your chair or on the floor.

Now imagine a sloping hill, low, still,

and heavy - softening to cover the land.

Muscles are at ease. Close eyes or stare gently.

Or try long blinks. You chose.

Breathe and **rest** for a little while.

Lesson Reflection for Teaching Mindful Moods

Highlights

What did students report / notice?

What did you notice, for you or for students?

Components

What aspects can you repeat as a practice, beyond the lesson?

What can you change to be more relevant for your students?

What can be tied in and integrated into other subjects or themes?

Planning, Spacing & Pacing

How did the timing play a role in the experience of the lesson?

What will you adjust for next lesson or next year?

Resources & Materials

What worked well?

What didn't quite fit?

What will you look for / research / have on hand next time?

What additional materials would be helpful for the next lesson?

And for this lesson next year?

Teacher Reflection

What is your overall impression of your experience of this lesson / module?

Module 4

Bump & Bounce Back

Mindful Message: We can view our set-backs as healthy, life lessons for gaining our own wisdom.

Preparation to Teach Module 4

LESSON & GOAL	SEL CONNECTION	TEACHING TOOLS	GoNoodle VIDEOS
Lesson 1 **Bumps & Set-Backs** Students recognize set-backs as useful and common for all.	Explore some of the emotions that can follow set-backs.	**Materials:** Chimes Book: *Alexander and the Terrible, Horrible, No Good, Very Bad Day* By Judith Viorst **Pre-Practice:** Belly Breath	**Videos:** FLOW – *Weather the Storm* THINK ABOUT IT – *Believe in Yourself*
Lesson 2 **Self-Talk** Students generate positive self-talk to create strength after a bump in life.	Develop strategies to support ourselves and others through set-backs.	**Materials:** Chimes Activity Sheet - *Bubbles & Advice* **Pre-Practice:** Cross-Your-Heart Breath	**Videos:** FLOW – *Weather the Storm* FLOW – *Chin Up* THINK ABOUT IT – *Be Kind*
Lesson 3 **Bounce Back** Students identify practices that strengthen their ability to bounce back.	Appreciate the strength we have and can build upon to bounce back.	**Materials:** Chimes Bouncy ball **Pre-Practice:** Open & Hug	**Videos:** FLOW – *Chin Up* FLOW – *Victorious* FLOW – *Up & Moving*
Lesson 4 **Begin Again** Students identify resilience strategies that will help them begin again.	Recognize and support the courage it takes to begin again.	**Materials:** Chimes Activity Sheets – *Mindful Strategies to Begin Again* **Pre-Practice:** Open & Hug	**Videos:** FLOW – *Begin Again* FLOW – *Victorious* THINK ABOUT IT – *You are Courage*

Teaching Components for Module 4

FOCUS	MINDFUL MOVES	EXPLORE	BALANCE & REST

Engage: Video option
 	
FLOW – *Weather the Storm*
 	
Attention: Pass the Chimes
 	
Breath: Cross-Your-Heart Breath
	Foot Work in Mindful Mountain
	Open & Hug
	Elevator Breath
	   with *Challenge
	Press & Let Go
	   with *Challenge
		Group Activity:
		
		Book – *Alexander and the Terrible… Day*
		
		Chalk Talk:
		Focus on story (book)
		
		Video:
		THINK ABOUT IT – *Believe in Yourself*
			Balance:
			
			Creative Balance
			
			Rest:
			
			Balloon Breath

Engage: Video option
 	
FLOW – *Weather the Storm*
 	
Attention: Pass the Chimes
 	
Breath: Cross-Your-Heart Breath
	Foot Work in Mindful Mountain
	Open & Hug
	Elevator Breath
	   with *Challenge
	Press & Let Go
	   with *Challenge
	
	Video:
	
	FLOW – *Chin Up*
		Think, Pair, Share:
		
		Activity Sheet - *Bubbles & Advice*
		
		Video:
		
		THINK ABOUT IT – *Be Kind*
			Balance:
			
			Creative Balance
			
			Rest:
			
			Balloon Breath

Engage: Video option
FLOW – *Chin Up*
 	
Attention: Gentle Chime
 	
Breath: Cross-Your-Heart Breath
	Mindful Mountain
	Bobble Head & Shoulders
	Open & Hug
	Elevator Breath
	   with *Challenge
	Press & Let Go
	   with *Challenge
	
	Video:
	
	FLOW – *Victorious*
		Group Activity:
		
		Pass the Bouncy Ball
		
		Video:
		
		FLOW – *Up & Moving*
			Balance:
			
			Creative Balance
			
			Rest:
			
			Balloon Breath
			   with *Challenge

Engage: Video option
 	
FLOW – *Begin Again*
 	
Attention: Gentle Chime
 	
Breath: Cross-Your-Heart Breath
	Mindful Mountain
	Bobble Head & Shoulders
	Open & Hug
	Elevator Breath
	   with *Challenge
	Press & Let Go
	   with *Challenge
	
	Video:
	
	FLOW – *Victorious*
		Solo Reflection:
		
		Activity Sheet - *Mindful Strategies to Begin Again*
		
		Video:
		
		THINK ABOUT IT – *You Are Courage*
			Balance:
			Creative Balance
			
			Rest:
			
			Balloon Breath
			   with *Challenge

| Module 4 **Bump & Bounce Back** | **Mindful Message:** We can view our set-backs as healthy, life lessons for gaining our own wisdom. |

Lesson 1 – Bumps & Set-backs

Goal: Students recognize set-backs as useful and common for all.

Pre-Practice:

Belly Breath

Materials:

- Chimes

Book – *Alexander and the Terrible, Horrible, No Good, Very Bad Day*

SEL Connection:

Explore some of the emotions that can follow set-backs.

GoNoodle Videos:

FLOW – *Weather the Storm*

THINK ABOUT IT – *Believe in Yourself*

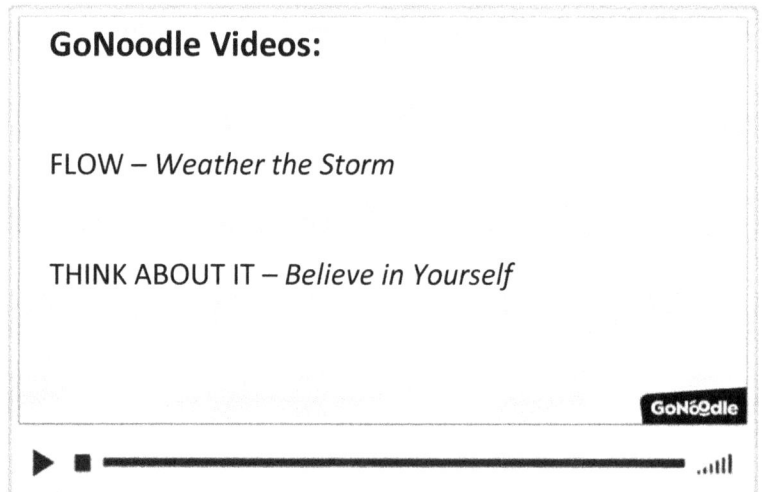

FOCUS

Engage: Video

FLOW – *Weather the Storm*

Attention: Pass the Chimes

Place your attention on the sound. Eyes might stare or close gently.

Ring Chime 1 time.

Pass chimes carefully to students.

Each may lead with a phrase to guide others.

Share helpful terms like: *Focus, Attention, Notice…*

Breath: Cross-Your-Heart Breath

Sit like a mindful mountain.

Cross forearms, fingertips rest on shoulders.

Breathe in and out, and notice arms moving

while your body breathes.

Repeat two times. Eyes might close to feel more.

MINDFUL MOVES

> We all get to move by CHOICE.
> Notice how your body feels and decide how to move.

Foot Work in Mindful Mountain

Sit comfortably. Raise one foot off the ground.

Leg might bend a little.

Circle (big toe) a few times slowly in each direction.

Point and flex the foot. Repeat. Slow then quick. Pause.

Return foot to floor. Try with other foot.

Body is still while feet move.

Open & Hug

Be a mindful mountain. Sit tall and calm.

Arms open wide to breathe in.

Then arms come around to cross, hug to exhale.

Next time your arms go wide, head looks up a little.

Breathing out - arms cross while head looks down,

    your back might round gently.

Repeat with 2 or 3 more breaths.

Elevator Breath*

Sit like a mindful mountain with shoulders down.

Place hands palm to palm, flat in front of your

    belly button.

Lift top (elevator) hand with inhale to top of head.

Exhale to float elevator hand down to rest on the other hand.

Switch hands if you wish.

* Challenge: This time try 0 to 4 as elevator rises, and slow your exhale

to count down from *6 to 0 as elevator descends.

Press and Let Go*

Mindful mountains sit tall.

Breathe in to press hands **forward**, with arms

    flat like the floor.

Breathe out to return arms and hands to sides, let go.

Breathe in to press **up**.

Breathe out to return, let go again, feel ease.

Breathe in to press *** down.**

Breathe out to return to ease.

Breathe in to press to each side, **wide**.

Breathe out to let go. Repeat sequence.

EXPLORE

Group Activity

Book:

Alexander and the Terrible, Horrible, No Good Very Bad Day

By Judith Viorst

Guide Question: invite verbal responses

"What does the title tell you?"

Sample answers: *he messes up on something, he forgets to do something, he feels unlucky…*

Read story.

Chalk Talk:

Guide Question: identify the kinds of setbacks (bumps in life) that happen for everyone – they are universal.

"What makes a day in your life hard to get through?"

Sample Answers: *forget homework, argument with siblings, chip a tooth at lunch…*

BALANCE

Creative Balance

Stand tall. Be a mountain.

Stare at a spot. Focus. Breathe.

Form a balancing shape.

It can be similar to others' OR

      unlike anyone else's.

Breathe, focus and be steady for 5, 4, 3, 2, 1.

Adjust and begin again, if needed.

Come back to Mountain on your own terms, with self-control.

Repeat.

REST

Balloon Breath

Sit tall with hands forming an imaginary

      balloon in front of belly.

Inhale to open and expand balloon hands **wide**.

Exhale to deflate balloon hands to original

      position.

Repeat two times, then sit back and **rest**.

Lesson Reflection for Teaching Mindful Moods

Highlights

What did students report / notice?

What did you notice, for you or for students?

Components

What aspects can you repeat as a practice, beyond the lesson?

What can you change to be more relevant for your students?

What can be tied in and integrated into other subjects or themes?

Planning, Spacing & Pacing

How did the timing play a role in the experience of the lesson?

What will you adjust for next lesson or next year?

Resources & Materials

What worked well?

What didn't quite fit?

What will you look for / research / have on hand next time?

What additional materials would be helpful for the next lesson?

And for this lesson next year?

Teacher Reflection

What is your overall impression of your experience of this lesson / module?

Module 4
Bump & Bounce Back

Mindful Message:
We can view our set-backs as healthy, life lessons for gaining our own wisdom.

Lesson 2 – Self-Talk

Goal: Students generate positive self-talk to create strength after a bump in life.

Materials:

- Chimes
- Activity Sheet – *Bubbles & Advice*

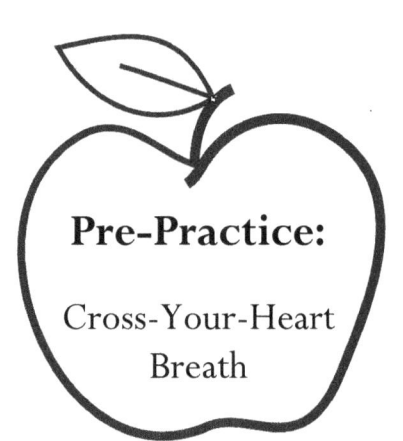

Pre-Practice:

Cross-Your-Heart Breath

SEL Connection:

Develop strategies to support ourselves and others through set-backs.

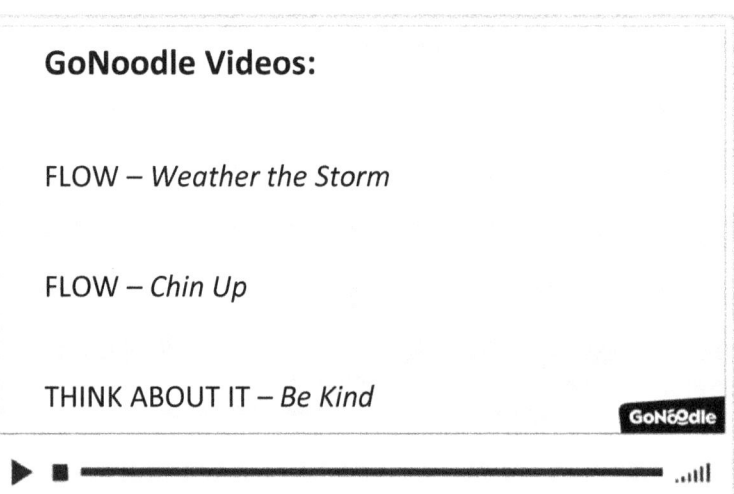

GoNoodle Videos:

FLOW – *Weather the Storm*

FLOW – *Chin Up*

THINK ABOUT IT – *Be Kind*

FOCUS

Engage: Video

FLOW — *Weather the Storm*

Attention: Pass the Chimes

Place your attention on the sound. Eyes stare or close.

Ring Chime 1 time.

Pass chimes carefully to students.

Each may lead with a phrase to guide others.

Share helpful terms like: *Focus, Attention, Notice…*

Breath: Cross-Your-Heart Breath

Sit like a mindful mountain.

Cross forearms with fingertips on shoulders.

Breathe in and out and notice arms moving
while your body breathes.

Repeat two times.

MINDFUL MOVES

We all get to move by CHOICE.
Notice how your body feels and decide how to move.

Foot Work in Mindful Mountain

Sit comfortably. Raise one foot off the ground.

Leg might bend a little.

Circle (big toe) a few times slowly in each direction.

Point and flex the foot. Repeat. Slow then fast. Pause.

Return foot to floor. Try with other foot.

Open & Hug

Be a mindful mountain, sit tall and calm.

Arms open wide to breathe in.

Then arms come around to cross, hug to exhale.

Next time arms go wide, look up a little.

Breathing out - arms cross while chin drops

    and your back might round.

Repeat with 2 or 3 more breaths.

GoNoodle Video:

FLOW – *Chin Up*

Elevator Breath*

Sit like a mindful mountain with shoulders down.

Place hands palm to palm, flat in front of your

    belly button.

Lift top (elevator) hand with inhale to top of head.

Exhale to float elevator hand down to rest on the other hand.

Switch hands if you wish. Repeat 2 more times.

    * Challenge: This time try counting from 0 to 4 as elevator rises, and

    lengthen your exhale to count down from *6 to 0 as your elevator descends.

Press and Let Go*

Mindful mountains sit tall. Try that.

Breathe in to press hands **forward**, with forearms

    flat like the floor.

Breathe out to return arms and hands to sides, let go.

Breathe in to press **up**.

Breathe out to return to ease, let go.

Breathe in to press * **down**. Breathe out to let go.

Breathe in to press to each side, **wide**.

Breathe out to let go.

* Challenge: Try pressing one forward and one back, let go. Then switch.

EXPLORE

Think, Pair, Share:

Activity Sheet – *Bubbles & Advice*

Write title on board: *a Conversation with a troubled Friend*

Hand out one Activity Sheet to each pair of students.

Guide Statements:

Imagine that a friend has made a mistake or had a set-back in his/her life. Write what the friend might be saying to themselves (self-talk) in the bubbles.

Write a few things you might say to show you care in the advice tags. Samples: "it's going to be okay," "I get it," "how can I help?"

Wrap-Up: In pairs, students **take turns** saying the phrases to each other.

Students can practice reading the phrases silently to themselves as Self Talk.

Reflection: Ask students for verbal reflections.

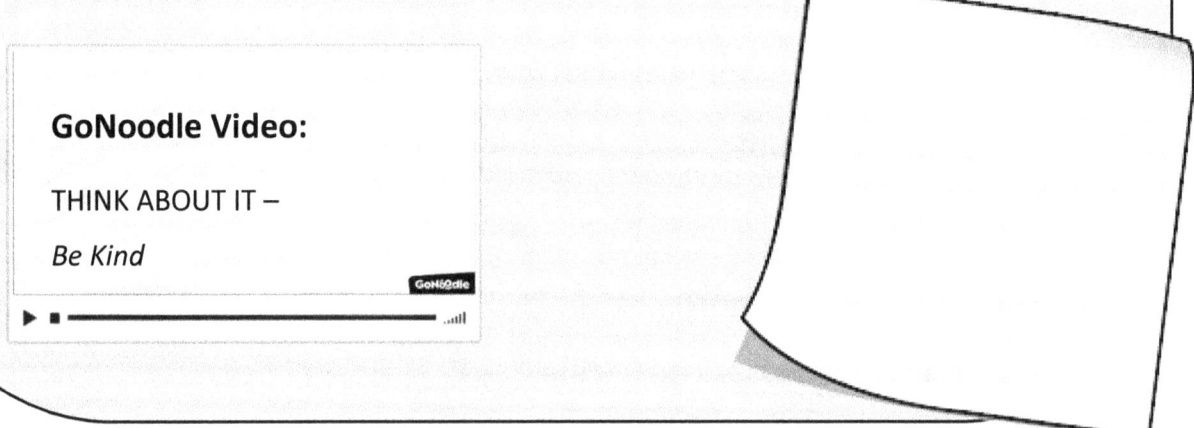

GoNoodle Video:

THINK ABOUT IT –

Be Kind

BALANCE

Creative Balance

Stand tall. Be a mountain.

Stare at a spot. Focus. Breathe.

Form a creative, balancing shape.

It can be like OR unlike anyone else.

Breathe, focus and remain steady for 5, 4, 3, 2, 1.

Adjust and begin again, if needed.

Come back to Mountain on your own terms, with self-control.

Repeat.

* Try to be steady longer: 10, 9, 8, 7, 6, 5, 4, 3, 2, 1, 0

REST

Balloon Breath

Sit tall with hands forming an imaginary balloon in front of your belly.

Inhale to open and expand balloon, hands go **wide**.

Exhale to deflate balloon hands to original, small balloon position.

Repeat two times then sit back and **rest**.

Lesson Reflection for Teaching Mindful Moods

Highlights

What did students report / notice?

What did you notice, for you or for students?

Components

What aspects can you repeat as a practice, beyond the lesson?

What can you change to be more relevant for your students?

What can be tied in and integrated into other subjects or themes?

Planning, Spacing & Pacing

How did the timing play a role in the experience of the lesson?

What will you adjust for next lesson or next year?

Resources & Materials

What worked well?

What didn't quite fit?

What will you look for / research / have on hand next time?

What additional materials would be helpful for the next lesson?

And for this lesson next year?

Teacher Reflection

What is your overall impression of your experience of this lesson / module?

| Module 4 **Bump & Bounce Back** | **Mindful Message:** We can view our set-backs as healthy, life lessons for gaining our own wisdom. |

Lesson 3 – Bounce Back

Goal: Students identify practices that strengthen their ability to bounce back.

Pre-Practice:

Open & Hug

Materials:

- Chimes
- Bouncy Ball

SEL Connection:

Appreciate the strength we have and can build upon to bounce back.

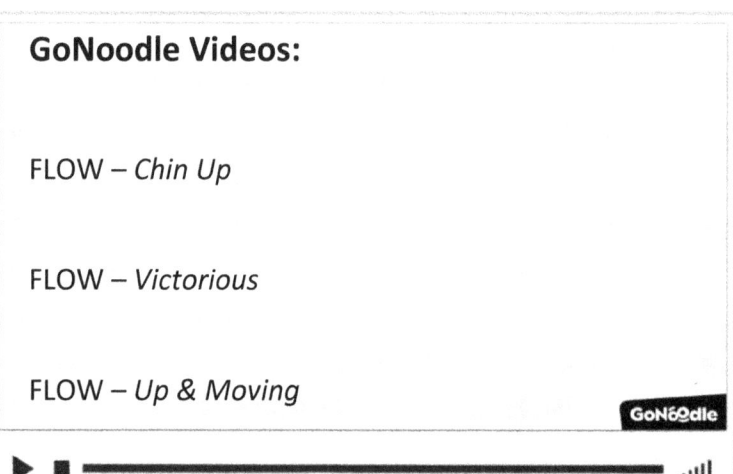

GoNoodle Videos:

FLOW – *Chin Up*

FLOW – *Victorious*

FLOW – *Up & Moving*

FOCUS

Engage: Video option

FLOW – *Chin Up*

Attention: Gentle Chime

Place your attention on the sound. Eyes stare or close.

Ring Chime 1 time.

This time the chime will be so soft that your attention will have to focus even more to stay with it.

Tap Chime as gently as possible.

Let's try an even softer sound. Challenge your attention.

Tap Chime to make the softest sound possible. Begin again if needed.

Breath: Cross-Your-Heart Breath

Sit like a mindful mountain.

Cross forearms with fingertips on shoulders.

Breathe in and out and notice arms moving

while your body breathes.

Repeat 2 times.

MINDFUL MOVES

We all get to move by CHOICE.
Notice how your body feels and decide how to move.

Mindful Mountain

Bobble Head & Shoulders

Carefully try Bobble Head series first.

Then shoulders lift, lower a couple of times.

Shoulders can circle (both then 1 at a time) in each direction.

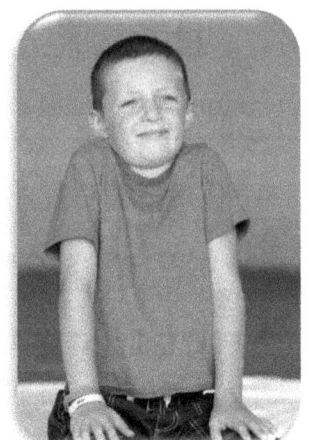

Open & Hug

Be a mindful mountain, sit tall and at ease.

Arms open wide to breathe in.

Then arms come around to cross and hug to exhale.

Next time arms go wide, head looks up a little.

Breathing out - arms cross while gazing

    down (a tiny bit).

Repeat with 2 or 3 more breaths.

*Maybe open with arms up and wide for more energy.

GoNoodle Video:

FLOW – *Victorious*

Elevator Breath*

Sit like a mindful mountain with shoulders down.

Place hands palm to palm, flat in front of your

belly button.

Lift top (elevator) hand with inhale to top of head.

Exhale to float elevator hand down to rest on the other hand.

Switch hands if you wish.

* Challenge: Take the elevator to the floor - when you exhale, let your elevator hand go past your belly hand and drop all the way to the actual floor.

Press and Let Go*

Mindful mountains sit tall. Be tall and still.

Breathe in to press hands **forward**, with forearms

are flat like the floor.

Breathe out to return arms and hands to sides, let go.

Breathe in to press **up**.

Breathe out to return to mountain, let go

Breathe in to press *** diagonally.**

Breathe out to return, let go. Diagonal to the other side.

Breathe in to press to each side, **wide**.

Breathe out to let go. Repeat the sequence and maybe add **down.**

EXPLORE

Group Activity:

Pass the Bouncy Ball

Write three-step process on the board:

1. Bounce — **name** setback/bump/error
2. Hold — **share** supportive Self Talk
3. Bounce Again — **identify** lesson learned

Teacher shares **brief example** of a school-related set-back/mistake/bump in the road, shares positive self-talk, and a lesson learned (model taking appropriate think-time).

Bounce the ball on floor **once** while naming it.

Sample ideas: *forgot lunch, locked keys in car, stubbed toe on desk leg…*

Hold the ball to share Self Talk phrase.

Sample phrase: *Wow, I must have been distracted, won't do that again, I can change that…*

Bounce ball again to identify lesson learned.

Pass the ball to students. Some may pass. It's okay.

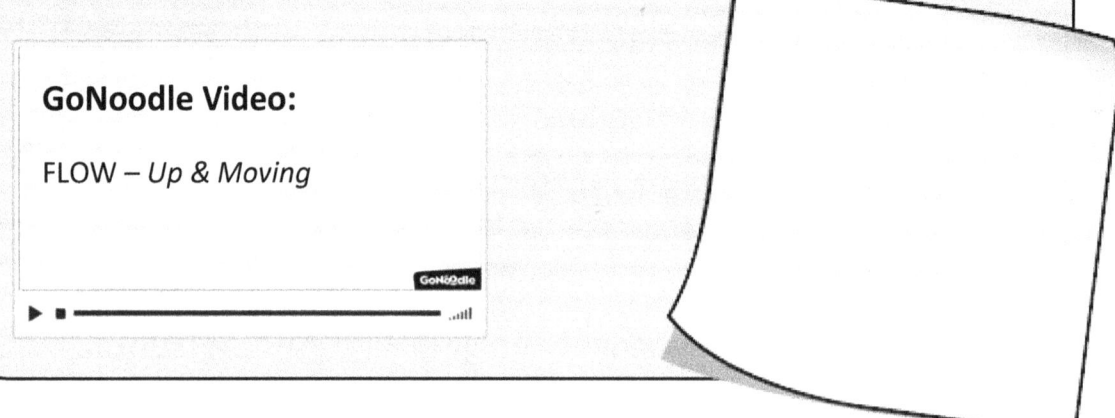

GoNoodle Video:

FLOW – *Up & Moving*

BALANCE

Creative Balance

Stand tall. Be a mountain.

Stare at a spot. Focus. Breathe.

Form a balancing shape.

It can be like OR unlike anyone else.

Breathe, focus and be steady for 5, 4, 3, 2, 1.

Adjust and begin again, if needed.

Come back to Mountain on your own terms, with self-control.

*Let a student lead with another creative balance.

　　Leader could speak to give others instruction or silently show them what to do.

REST

Balloon Breath*

Sit tall with hands forming an imaginary

　　balloon in front of belly.

Inhale to open and expand balloon hands **tall***.

Exhale to deflate balloon hands to original

　　position.

Repeat 2 times then sit back and **rest**.

Lesson Reflection for Teaching Mindful Moods

<u>Highlights</u>

What did students report / notice?

What did you notice, for you or for students?

<u>Components</u>

What aspects can you repeat as a practice, beyond the lesson?

What can you change to be more relevant for your students?

What can be tied in and integrated into other subjects or themes?

<u>Planning, Spacing & Pacing</u>

How did the timing play a role in the experience of the lesson?

What will you adjust for next lesson or next year?

Resources & Materials

What worked well?

What didn't quite fit?

What will you look for / research / have on hand next time?

What additional materials would be helpful for the next lesson?

And for this lesson next year?

Teacher Reflection

What is your overall impression of your experience of this lesson / module?

| Module 4 **Bump & Bounce Back** | **Mindful Message:** We can view our set-backs as healthy, life lessons for gaining our own wisdom. |

Lesson 4 – Begin Again

Goal: Students identify resilience strategies that will help them begin again.

Pre-Practice:

Open & Hug

Materials:

- Chimes
- Activity Sheet —*Mindful Strategies to Begin Again*.

SEL Connection:

Recognize and support the courage to begin again.

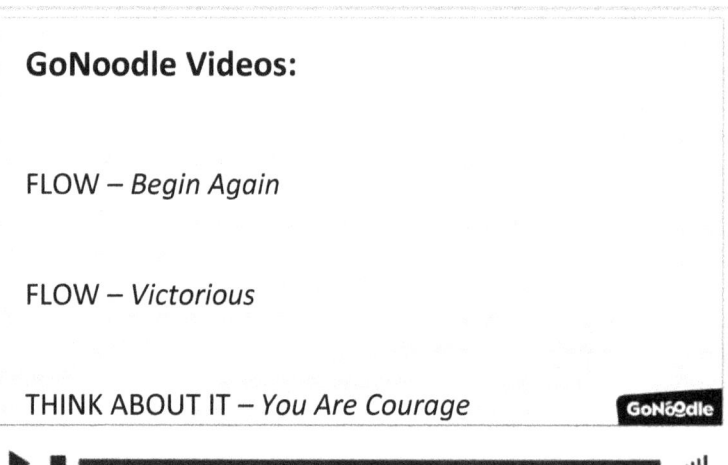

GoNoodle Videos:

FLOW – *Begin Again*

FLOW – *Victorious*

THINK ABOUT IT – *You Are Courage*

FOCUS

Engage: Video option

FLOW – *Begin Again*

Attention: Gentle Chime

Rest your attention on the sound. Eyes stare or gently close.

Ring Chime 1 time.

This time the chime will be so soft that your attention will have to focus so carefully to stay with it.

Tap Chime as gently as possible.

Let's try an even softer sound. Challenge your attention.

Tap Chime to make the softest sound possible.

Breath: Cross-Your-Heart Breath

Sit like a mindful mountain.

Cross forearms with fingertips on shoulders.

Breathe in and out, and notice arms moving while your body breathes. Repeat 3 times.

MINDFUL MOVES

We all get to move by CHOICE.
Notice how your body feels and decide how to move.

Mindful Mountain

Bobble Head & Shoulders

Carefully try Bobble Head series first (chin up & down, turns, tilt).

Then shoulders lift, lower a couple of times.

Shoulders can circle (both then 1 at a time) in each direction.

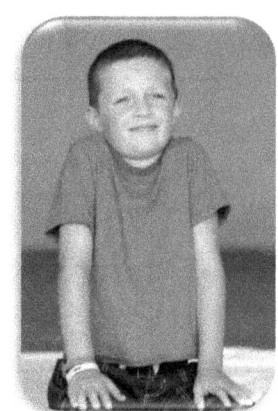

Open & Hug

Be a mindful mountain, sit tall and calm.

Arms open wide to breathe in.

Then arms come around to cross, hug to exhale.

Next time arms go wide, head looks up a little.

Breathing out - arms cross, maybe look down.

Repeat with 2 or 3 more breaths.

*Try remaining crossed and rounded for 2 breaths.

   Not tight, just crossed and rounded.

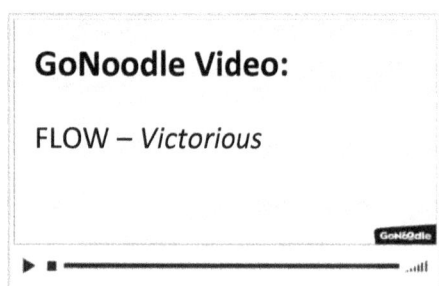

GoNoodle Video:

FLOW – *Victorious*

Elevator Breath*

Sit like a mindful mountain with shoulders down.

Place hands palm to palm, flat in front of your

belly button.

Lift top (elevator) hand with inhale to top of head.

Exhale to float elevator hand down to rest on the other hand.

Switch hands if you wish.

* Challenge: Take the elevator to the Floor - When you exhale, let your elevator

hand go past your belly hand and drop all the way to the actual floor.

Press and Let Go*

Mindful mountains sit tall.

Breathe in to press hands **forward**, with arms

flat like the floor.

Breathe out to return arms and hands to sides, let go.

Breathe in to press **up**.

Breathe out to return, let go

Breathe in to press * **diagonally**.

Breathe out to return, let go. Open to the other side too.

Breathe in to press to each side, **wide**. Breathe out to let go.

*Try pressing back, fingertips down. Exhale to create ease, then rest.

EXPLORE

Solo Reflection:

Activity Sheet – *Mindful Strategies to Begin Again*

Guide Statement:

Think or imagine a time when you had a rough moment or day - a set-back, a bump in your life.

Now, think back on our mindful activities, attention and breath practices, movements, or videos - strategies we've tried in Mindful Moods.

Guide Question:

As you imagine bouncing back from rough times, what ideas have been or would be helpful to help you begin again? Write ideas on sticky notes.

Sample Answers:

- Breathing out
- Stretching and yawning
- Doing fun balances with friends
- Finding a sound to pay attention to
- Trying some videos at home

Reflect and Share.

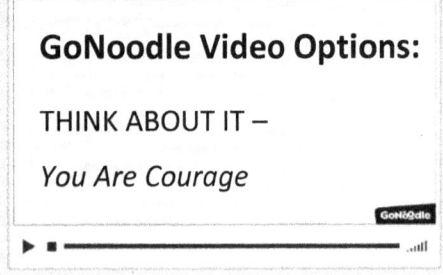

GoNoodle Video Options:

THINK ABOUT IT –

You Are Courage

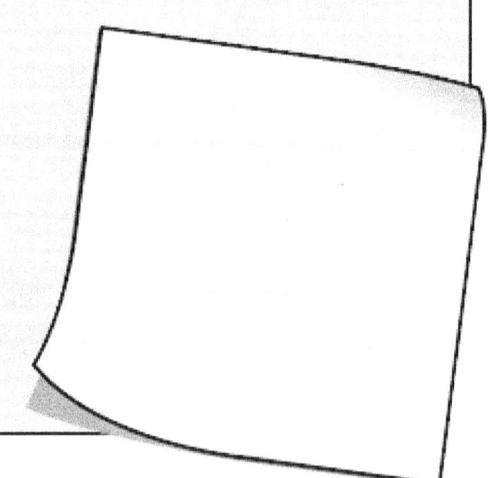

BALANCE

Creative Balance*

Stand tall. Be a mountain.

Stare at a spot. Focus. Breathe.

Form a balancing shape.

　　*Then maybe one that feels **open.**

　　*Try one that is **closed**. How about a moving version?

Adjust and begin again, if needed.

Come back to Mountain on your own terms.

Repeat and change. Make new categories: _____

Have fun with these balances.

REST

Balloon Breath*

Sit tall with hands forming an imaginary

　　balloon in front of belly.

Inhale to open and expand balloon

　　hands **diagonally***.

Exhale to deflate balloon hands to original position.

Repeat with other ideas and then sit back to **rest**.

Lesson Reflection for Teaching Mindful Moods

Highlights

What did students report / notice?

What did you notice, for you or for students?

Components

What aspects can you repeat as a practice, beyond the lesson?

What can you change to be more relevant for your students?

What can be tied in and integrated into other subjects or themes?

Planning, Spacing & Pacing

How did the timing play a role in the experience of the lesson?

What will you adjust for next lesson or next year?

Resources & Materials

What worked well?

What didn't quite fit?

What will you look for / research / have on hand next time?

What additional materials would be helpful for the next lesson?

And for this lesson next year?

Teacher Reflection

What is your overall impression of your experience of this lesson / module?

Activity Sheets

Feathers & Stones

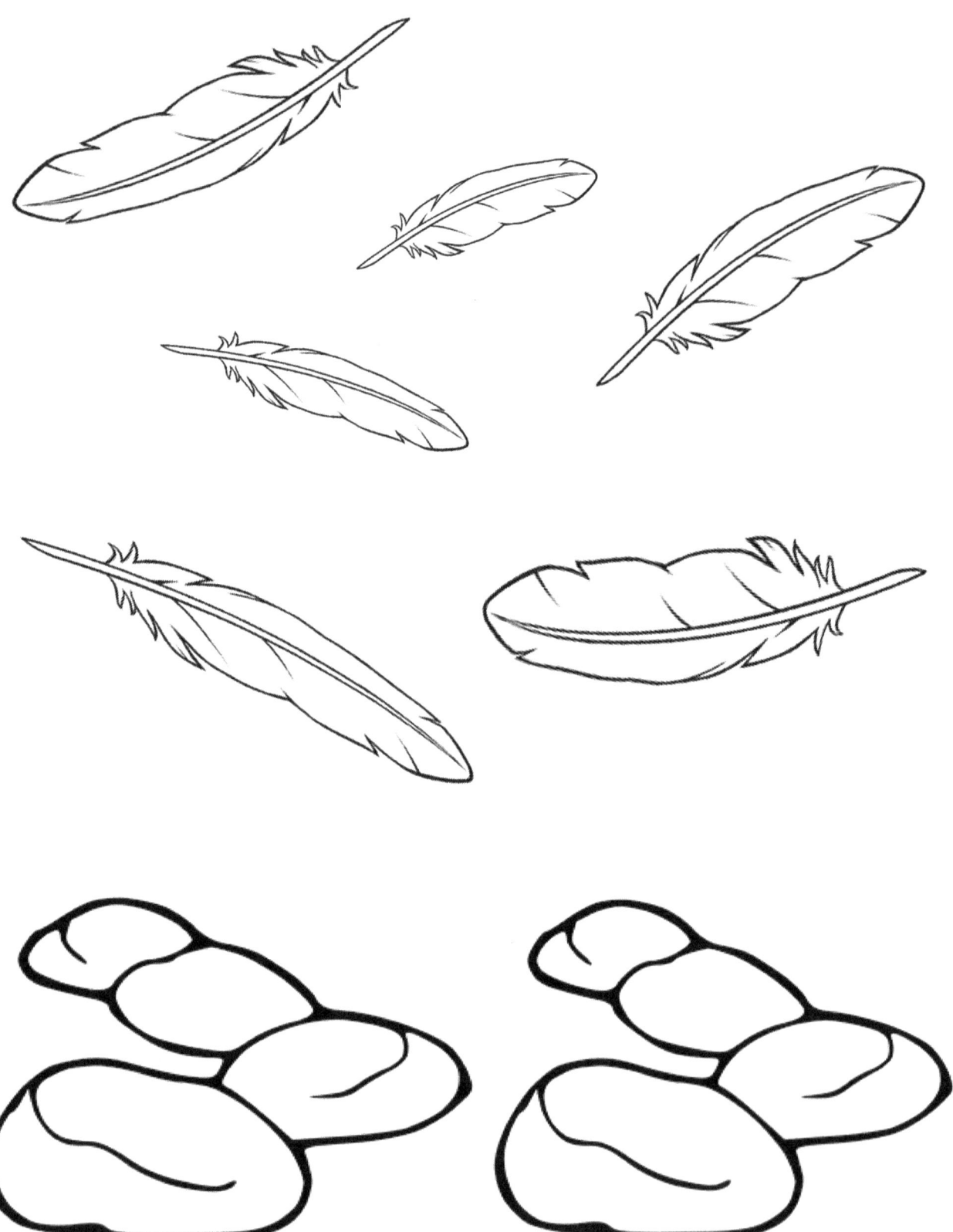

Emotional Body Map

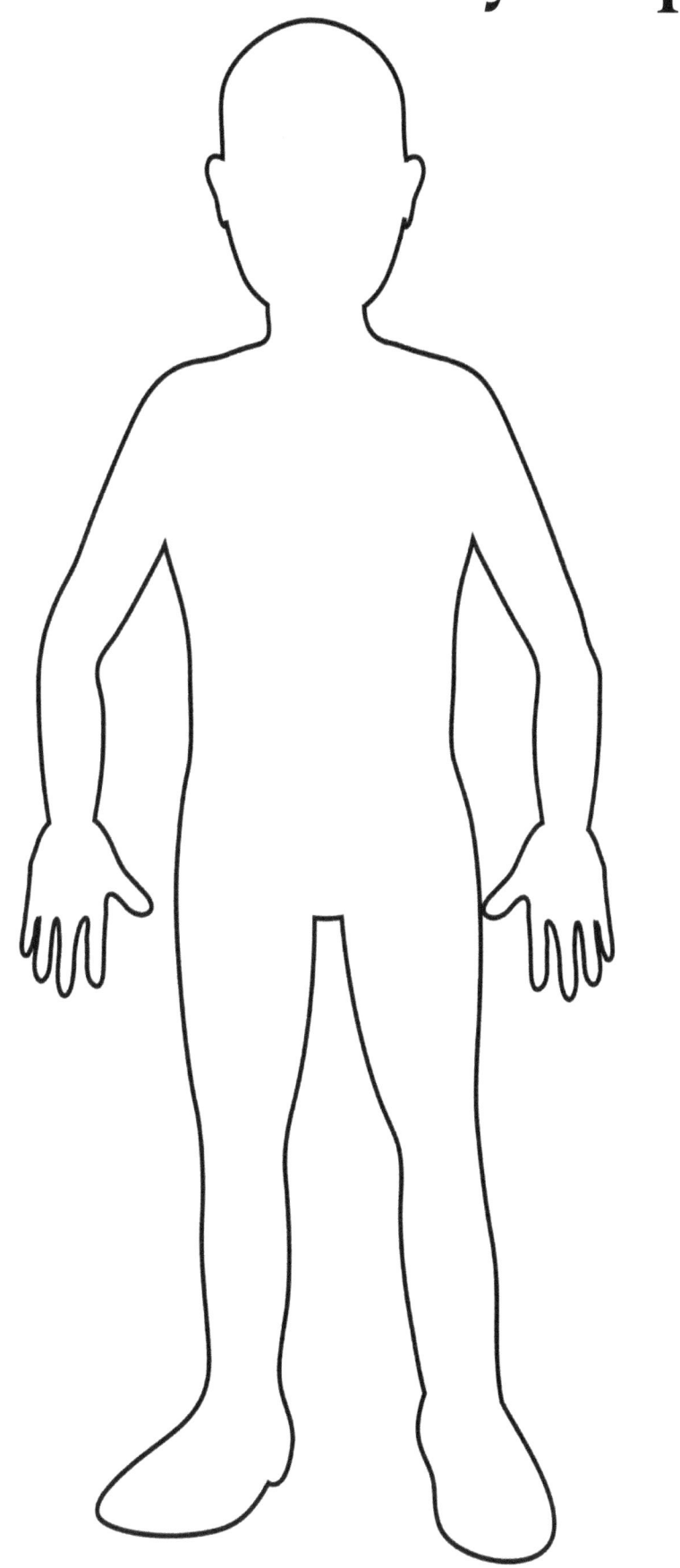

Worry Clouds

Bubbles & Advice

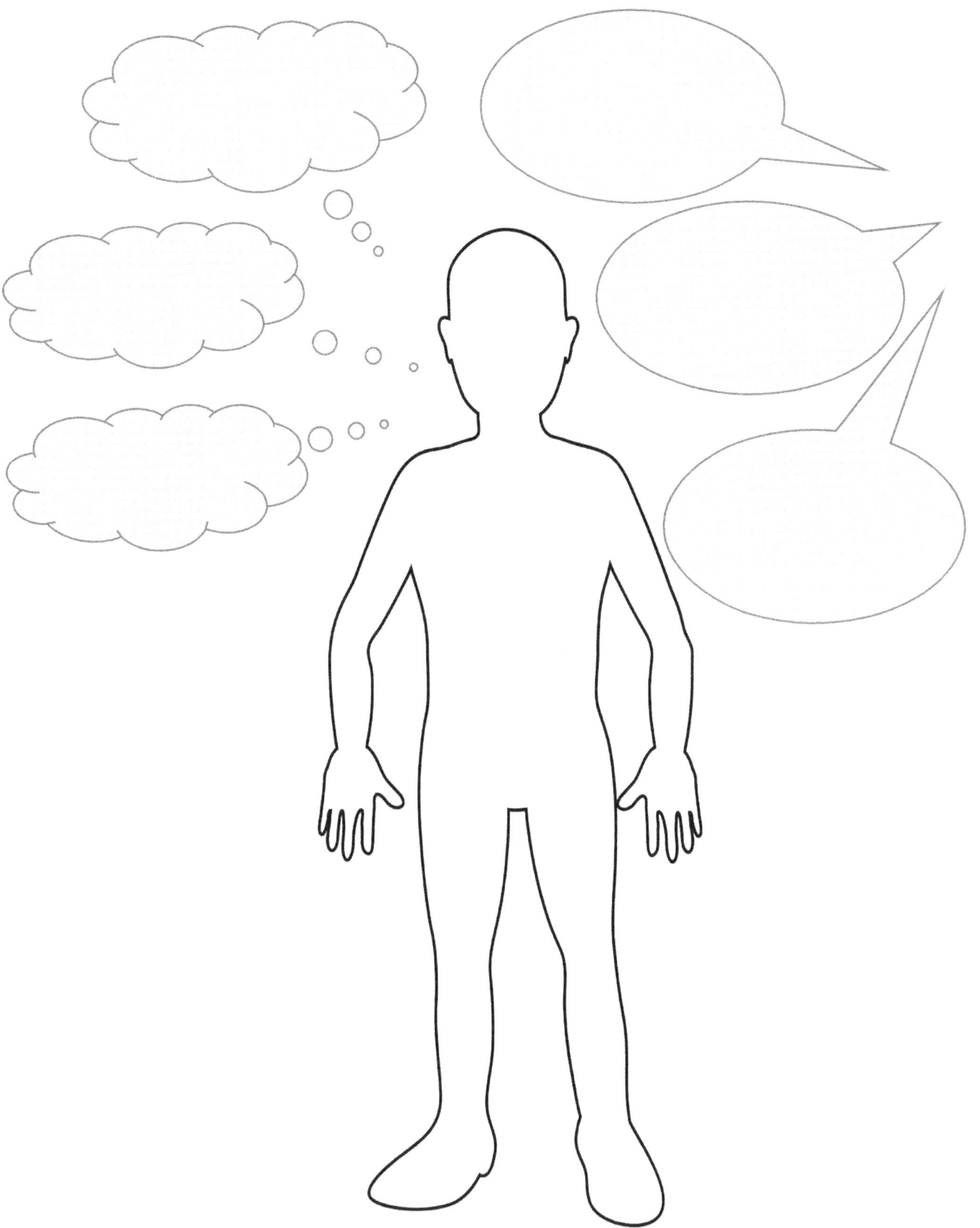

Mindful Strategies to Begin Again

Mindful Moods Supplement

add **positive mindsets** to lessons with

I Am ~ I Can:
365 Affirmations for Kids

Module I: It's All You (self-awareness and introduction to mindful practices)

Lesson Theme	I Am ~ I Can
1. Aware	p. 34-35
2. Awake	p. 36-37
3. Care	p. 12-13
4. Rest	p. 22-23

Module II: Name It & Tame It (get to know emotions and how they can be managed)

Lesson Theme	I Am ~ I Can
1. Name It	p. 14-15 and 70-71 (Feelings Index)
2. Weight It	p. 10-11
3. Feel It	p. 26-27
4. Tame It	p. 54-55

Module III: Helpful Emotions (emotions communicate what is going on inside)

Lesson Theme	I Am ~ I Can
1. Emotions Speak	p. 18-19
2. Angry Fists	p. 64-65
3. Worried Belly	p. 28-29
4. Knots of Emotions	p. 24-25

Module IV: Bump & Bounce Back (with support, resilience can be a learnable skill)

Lesson Theme	I Am ~ I Can
1. Bumps & Set-Backs	p. 50-51
2. Self-Talk	p. 8-9
3. Bounce Back	p. 38-39
4. Begin Again	p. 30-31

Resources: Mindfulness for Schools

Mobile Apps

Calm.com: Website and mobile app with guided mindfulness and relaxation exercises. Free for Teachers.

Insight Timer: Free mobile app with virtual "bells" and guided audio to support your practice.

Headspace: This popular app has a free introductory period.

GoNoodleKids: FREE Mobile App, kid-safe. Kids can try the free Games App too.

Guided Mindfulness

MindfullyADD.com: research, relevant articles, and audio practices for teens and up.

Mindful.org: "Audio Resources for Guided Meditations" collection: Online, free, guided practices.

Mindfulness for Elementary Classrooms

GoNoodle.com: FREE brain breaks, Mindful channels: FLOW, Think About It, Maximo

Stop, Breathe, Think for Kids: Guided practices for kids and classrooms.

Mindfulness Books for Educators

Wynne Kinder, M.Ed., *Peace Work for K-2 (2017), Mindful Choices for grades 6-8 (2018), Mindful Tools for Teens (2020), The Re-Set Process: Trauma-Informed Behavior Strategies with Dyane Carrere M.Ed. (2020), CALM: Mindfulness for Kids (book/cards 2019), I am ~ I can: 365 Affirmations for Kids (book/cards 2020)*

Patricia Jennings, *Mindfulness for Teachers (2015)*

Susan Kaiser Greenland, *The Mindful Child: How to Help Your Kid Manage Stress and Become Happier, Kinder and More Compassionate (2010) and Mindful Games (2017)*

Jon Kabat-Zinn, *Mindfulness for Beginners: Reclaiming the Present Moment - and Your Life*

Meena Srinivasan, *Teach, Breathe, Learn: Mindfulness in and out of the Classroom (2016)*

Christopher Willard and Mitch Abblett, *Growing Mindful: A Deck of Mindfulness Practices for All Ages*

Daniel Siegel, M.D. and Tina Payne Bryson, Ph.D., *The Whole-Brain Child*

Wellness Works in Schools

Wellness Works in Schools Curriculum and corresponding online trainings:

- Peace Work: Mindful Lessons of Self-Regulation for a Child's Early Years (grades PreK to 2)
- Mindful Moods: A Mindful, Social Emotional Learning Curriculum for Grades 3-5
- Mindful Choices: A Mindful, Social Emotional Learning Curriculum for Grades 6-8
- Mindful Tools for Teens (coming soon) Grades 9 to 12

www.wellnessworksinschools.com

Wynne Kinder, M. Ed.

Wynne's teaching career spans 30 years. The first half she spent in her own classrooms from kindergarten to 6th grade. While the second half has focused on bringing mindfulness and trauma-informed strategies into regular, special, and alternative education classrooms (K-12) through her program Wellness Works in Schools.

Wynne is the author of I Am ~ I Can: 365 Affirmations for Kids and CALM: Mindfulness for Kids through DK (Penguin Random House). Her four mindful curriculum programs & trainings for PreK-12 classrooms are: Peace Work, Mindful Moods*, Mindful Choices, and Mindful Tools for Teens incorporate helpful links or content she authored like GoNoodle's mindful channels FLOW, Think About It, and SEL BRAZER Fresh.

Wynne's teacher-supporting work includes online curriculum training, co-authoring The Re-Set Process & Related Trauma-Informed Behavior Strategies with Dyane Carrere (through Brookes Publishing – October 2020) and co-creating / teaching graduate certificate courses: Trauma, Restoration & Resilience in Educational Environments and Self-Care & Resilience for Educators at Eastern Mennonite University. www.wynnekinder.com

Books by Wynne Kinder

www.ingramcontent.com/pod-product-compliance
Lightning Source LLC
Chambersburg PA
CBHW080546170426
43195CB00016B/2692